MW01125515

THE WILD LIVES OF REPTILES AND AMPHIBIANS

Kathie and Ed Cox Jr.
Books on Conservation Leadership,
sponsored by The Meadows Center for Water
and the Environment, Texas State University

THE WILD LIVES OF REPTILES AND AMPHIBIANS

A Young Herpetologist's Guide

Michael A. Smith

Texas A&M University Press | College Station

Copyright © 2020 by Michael A. Smith
All rights reserved
First edition

This paper meets the requirements
of ANSI/NISO Z39.48–1992 (Permanence of Paper).
Binding materials have been chosen for durability.

Manufactured in Canada at Friesens

Library of Congress Cataloging-in-Publication Data

Names: Smith, Michael, 1951 April 18– author.
Title: The wild lives of reptiles and amphibians: a young herpetologist's
    guide / Michael A. Smith.
Other titles: Kathie and Ed Cox Jr. books on conservation leadership.
Description: First edition. | College Station: Texas A&M University Press,
    [2020] | Series: Kathie and Ed Cox Jr. books on conservation leadership
    | Includes bibliographical references and index. | Audience: Ages 13 |
    Audience: Grades 7–9 | Summary: "This introductory guide offers an
    educational and inspirational starting point to discovering reptiles and
    amphibians in their natural habitats by introducing readers to the
    exciting native species they can encounter on a family nature trip or a
    walk through the local park"—Provided by publisher.
Identifiers: LCCN 2019045917 (print) | LCCN 2019045918 (ebook) | ISBN
    9781623498733 | ISBN 9781623498740 (ebook)
Subjects: LCSH: Herpetology—Juvenile literature.
Classification: LCC QL644.2 .S623 2020 (print) | LCC QL644.2 (ebook) |
    DDC 597.9—dc23
LC record available at https://lccn.loc.gov/2019045917
LC ebook record available at https://lccn.loc.gov/2019045918

To Rick Pratt,
a mentor and great friend
from my early days,
and to
Elijah Lineman,
whose first nature explorations I
have been privileged to share.

Contents

Preface

We human beings are wired to be curious about the world around us, and we have more ways to explore and learn than ever before. In addition to getting out and experiencing things firsthand, we can listen to the stories others tell, or read a book. Thanks to the invention of cameras and sound recorders, we can look at images and listen to sounds from anywhere on earth and beyond. And now, of course, the internet constantly floods us with material. Never before have there been as many ways to feed our sense of curiosity. I still believe in the power of books to inspire our imagination and learning, and I wrote this one to focus our attention on some animals whose lives are often misunderstood. It is as if I'm tapping you on the shoulder, saying, "Excuse me, but there's something over here you might want to see."

Naturally, we are more preoccupied with our own species than with the other kinds of life on earth. We know countless things about social media, television, the layout of the city in which we live, how to use a credit card, things cats do on YouTube, how to balance a mathematical equation, the risks of identity theft—but we may not know the names of even a couple of the trees growing nearby, or where soil comes from, or how wetlands can filter and clean water. You know the names of several animals at the zoo, but can you name five of the ones living at a nearby creek? My bet is that we will live richer lives if we do not lose the connection with the natural world around us. Despite all the things we construct and manufacture, the things that really make life possible are the rivers, the soil, the air we breathe, the insects that pollinate our crops, and many other things that nature provides. This book is an effort to pass along knowledge of, and strengthen our connection to, the natural world.

But why focus on reptiles and amphibians, if my goal is to increase our overall connection with nature? One answer is that these are the animals I know best. But a more important answer is that reptiles and amphibians ("herps") are as beautiful, fascinating, and valuable as any other wildlife, despite how often people respond to them with fear or revulsion. They provide benefits such as helping control rodent and insect populations, and in turn they are a significant source of food for other animals. Their venoms have given us a variety of medicines, such as the ACE inhibitors used to treat high blood pressure and congestive heart failure. One other consideration is this: we need nature with all its parts, not just the pieces we are fond of. When we tinker with the natural world, taking out a species here, destroying places there, we risk disrupting things in ways we can't imagine. All the pieces in nature are connected, and changing one thing may in turn change something else. It is like trying to work on our car at the same time that we're driving it down the road. We can take out a part here, loosen something there, and maybe the car will keep going, but it will begin to run badly or even fall apart.

As I indicated, I want to strengthen our connection to the natural world while focusing on reptiles and amphibians. I want to do that by putting you, the reader, in the places where these animals live and then telling some of the stories of their daily lives. Understanding how they live is at least as interesting and rewarding as knowing what they look like and how to identify them. I also want to encourage you to spend time in the field. That is a great place to learn about these creatures and to clearly see the connections between herp and habitat. For some of us, a turtle is most fully a turtle in the place it lives. It is the same with a frog or a snake. Each animal needs the things it eats, the places it shelters or explores, and even the predators that eat it—all of these things have shaped what that frog or snake is and what it looks like. Maybe it has an athletic body for making an escape, or a pattern that looks like the grasses or leaves of its home for camouflage. Perhaps it has an upturned nose for digging through sandy soil, or crushing jaw surfaces so it can eat things with hard shells. You can't love that individual herp without loving the places that made it. It is that love for whole communities of animals and plants that motivates this book.

Acknowledgments

The idea for this book originated in a conversation with Stacy Eisenstark, an editor (at Texas A&M University Press at that time) with whom Clint King and I worked on the publication of our book *Herping Texas: The Quest for Reptiles and Amphibians*. The discussion with Ms. Eisenstark was about writing for middle school readers (and older), and her encouragement was very helpful. I appreciate the support of Emily Seyl and others at TAMU Press as the book made its way through the editorial process.

Once the project started, I depended as always on the understanding and support of my wife, Jo, as I spent many weekends and evenings obsessed with finding just the right words to describe some aspect of snake behavior or turtle hibernation.

My friend Jack Jeansonne was a natural choice as an illustrator, and working with him has been a real pleasure. I believe his illustrations will help make clear such things as turtle necks, snake venom glands, and rattlesnake rattles in ways my words cannot.

I owe a great deal to a number of people who read through part or all of the manuscript and offered helpful comments. Those people include Jo Smith, Kenedy Millikan, Viviana Ricardez, Rob Denkhaus, John Karges, Tim Cole, Carl Franklin, Bill Brooks, and Troy Hibbitts. Many thanks to Viviana, Carl, Troy, Richard Kostecke, and Justin Michels for contributing photos. I also want to thank Ki Rendon for letting me photograph her showing how to use a snake hook, and Embry Gabriel for allowing me to photograph her taking a photo of a Great Plains Ratsnake. Tim Cole was kind enough to rouse one of his Gila Monsters at the end of hibernation so I could photograph it. Many thanks to Jim Harrison and Kristen Wiley for the time I've been able to spend with them, learning more about venomous snakes and snakebite.

As I mention in chapter 8, my debt to the folks at the Fort Worth Children's Museum in the 1960s is immeasurable. John R. Preston and Rick Pratt set me on the right course (and any deviations from it have been entirely my fault). In later years, the guidance and support of Rob Denkhaus, Suzanne Tuttle, and others at the Fort Worth Nature Center & Refuge have been the perfect mix of mentoring and friendship. I also want to recognize the late Steve Campbell, who launched the Dallas–Fort Worth Herpetological Society with me at the end of 1999. He and I shared many great days in the field, and his support for my writing meant a lot.

THE WILD LIVES OF REPTILES AND AMPHIBIANS

CHAPTER 1

Introduction

"You Want to Go Snake Hunting?"

One day in mid-March 2018, a friend and I visited a small ranch northeast of Abilene. It was warm even though there were still a few days of winter left, and we were eager to see our first snake of the year. On a brushy, rocky hillside we got our wish. A Western Diamond-backed Rattlesnake about four feet long was sunning himself near the top of the hill. My friend Clint was just above him and was able to prevent the snake's getaway, using a snake hook to catch a loop of his body and pull him back out in the open. And so the serpent sat and rattled and waited, testing the air with his glossy black tongue. I was standing in a small ravine at eye level with the rattlesnake, getting my camera ready. I used my own snake hook to gently move a coil away from his head, trying not to add to his stress. This was not only for the snake's well-being but also for mine. If he blindly attempted another escape and came down into the ravine with me, I was going to have a little stress of my own. Having a four-foot-long frightened rattlesnake at my feet while balancing on loose rocks would not be a good situation. Everything worked out fine—we took a few photos while the snake buzzed and watched us, and then we left him to enjoy the sunny West Texas day.

Going out to see the first snake is one of my favorite rituals of

The Western Diamond-backed Rattlesnake we saw in March 2018 (photo by the author)

spring. Why is that? How does a person come to have a lifelong interest in reptiles and amphibians? Even though it is not how I make a living, this interest has taken me all over my home state of Texas to see most of the species that live in the wetlands, woods, prairies, and deserts (and that is the subject of an earlier book, *Herping Texas*,[1] that I wrote with Clint King). What is it about reptiles and amphibians that could inspire such curiosity and love for the animals and the places they live? The purpose of this book is to try to answer that question.

Here is a little bit about how it began for me. Sometime in about 1961, I was playing beside our house in Arvada, a suburb of Denver, Colorado. I had developed a big interest in dinosaurs, imagining great lumbering stegosaurs and menacing tyrannosaurs. However, I hadn't given much thought to the modern reptiles that might be living in my own neighborhood. That changed when the girl across the street showed up with a paper bag and said, "You want to go snake hunting?" We wandered the fields and a little creek and found a gartersnake. It was likely a Plains Gartersnake but could have been a Wandering Gartersnake; I don't have a photo or a clear picture in my mind. Whichever kind it was, that snake sent me down a path I am still on today, looking for snakes and other reptiles and amphibians.

Lots of other kids have similar stories, although the details may be different. At some point while growing up, you run across an animal that sets your imagination on fire, and your curiosity and intellect burn with the desire for more. For some people, the path leads to advanced training at a university and a career as a herpetologist (a scientist who studies reptiles and amphibians)

A Plains Gartersnake (photo by Justin D. Michels)

or wildlife biologist. Others may become zookeepers, taking care of exotic or rare animals or breeding them in zoo conservation programs. And for some, like me, reptiles and amphibians become a hobby, a passionate interest, or a sort of second career. This book is for any of those folks, the ones who are starting down the path and could use a good guide to what reptiles and amphibians are, how they live, and how we might see them up close in the wild.

A Quick Look at What Is a "Reptile" and an "Amphibian"

On that first walk back in 1961, one of the things Sherry and I found in that creek was a "horsehair snake." Neither of us was entirely sure if it really was some sort of snake, but this animal is actually a worm that resembles a thick strand of hair, like from the mane of a horse. It was definitely not a snake! Snakes, like other reptiles, are vertebrates, meaning that they have a bony skeleton with a backbone. Snakes are closely related to lizards. Other reptiles include turtles, crocodilians like alligators and crocodiles, and the tuatara, which looks kind of like a lizard and lives on islands off the coast of New Zealand. All of them have scales as part of their skin, breathe air, and either have four legs or are descended from animals with four legs. There is one other group of animals that technically falls under that umbrella of related animals that we call reptiles: birds! They are among the descendants of the dinosaurs, even though most people do not think of birds as reptiles. For our purposes, in this book we do not include birds in our discussion of reptiles. No offense, birds! We really do like seeing you in the field.

What about frogs? They have skeletons, breathe air (as adults), have four legs, and are cold-blooded just like reptiles. Although most people know the term "cold-blooded," the better term for this is *ectothermic*. The "thermic" part of it refers to temperature, and the "ecto" part means outside. That is, their bodies get heat from things outside them, like sunshine or warm water, not from inside. Frogs and salamanders are amphibians, along with the legless, tropical caecilians, which do not occur in the United States. One way they differ from reptiles is that they lay eggs without shells, and those eggs are mostly laid in water and hatch into aquatic *larvae* that breathe through gills. Later, the larvae transform into land-dwelling adults—with a few exceptions. Additionally, instead of dry and scaly skin, their skin is fairly delicate and may be slimy or warty. We will talk more about how amphibians and reptiles are similar and different in later chapters.

Herpetology and "Herps"

The study of reptiles and amphibians is called *herpetology*, which comes from the Greek words "herpeton," meaning a creeping thing, and "logos," referring to study. That is, herpetology is the study of "creeping things." Reptiles and amphibians are called "herpetofauna," and a shorter version of that name is "herps." You might not have heard the word "herpetofauna," because it is much easier to just say "herps." Also, if you are looking for herps, you are "herping."

Herpetology is one branch of the science of biology. What does it mean to say that it is the "scientific study" of herps? When we want to answer some question about these animals, we use what we already know to form a sort of educated guess that could answer our question (in science this is called a "hypothesis"). Then we figure out how to put our hypothesis to the test and do lots of observations to see what the results tell us. This is basically what an experiment is: using careful observations to test whether our educated guess is correct. If our observations do not confirm what we thought, we figure out a different explanation that we can test—a different hypothesis. Science is a set of tools for exploring the world around us. We use those tools to learn more, correct our mistaken beliefs, and help us understand the world better.

Suppose we want to know why some species of snakes eat one kind of food and not another—are baby snakes born wanting to eat certain things, or do they learn it? Years ago, Gordon

Burghardt thought that the way to figure this out was to use newborn snakes that had not yet been around anything they might eat. He presented the scents of different possible foods on cotton swabs and noted how many times the baby snake tongue-flicked each swab. Tongue-flicking allows snakes to pick up scents, and when they tongue-flick a lot, that shows interest. But baby snakes will tongue-flick out of curiosity, even if the swab is unscented. So how do we know just how many tongue-flicks mean "Hey, I want to eat that!" and not just "What's this?" Dr. Burghardt made sure that one of the swabs had been dipped in distilled water, so it had no scent. In the language of scientific experiments, this was a control condition, letting him know how many tongue-flicks were just responses to the swab itself. Anything above that value meant that the snake was showing interest in the smell. In one of his experiments, he demonstrated that baby Graham's Crawfish Snakes and Queensnakes are born with a taste for crayfish (which is what the adults mostly eat), while Northern Watersnakes are born with an interest in amphibians and fish for dinner.[2] A simple but carefully designed experiment taught us something important about these snakes.

Scientific Names

When I talked about finding a rattlesnake in March 2018, I used the English name, "Western Diamond-backed Rattlesnake." It refers to one specific kind of snake. This snake also has another name, *Crotalus atrox*, which is what herpetologists would call it when they wanted to be clear and accurate. It is that snake's scientific name, in which *Crotalus* refers to a group of rattlesnakes (that group is called a genus) and *atrox* refers to the particular kind (or species) of snake within the group. Scientific names show the way we understand different animals to be related. For example, *Crotalus horridus* is a rattlesnake that is related to *Crotalus atrox*; you can tell because they share the name *Crotalus*. When you look in field guides, you will notice that scientific names change from time to time as we learn more about how these animals are related. The ratsnake in chapter 4 used to be in the genus *Elaphe*, but now that genus is *Pantherophis*. In addition to the name for its species, it had a third name, a subspecies name, that showed that it was in a population of *obsoleta* ratsnakes that was a little different from the others. So it was *Elaphe obsoleta lindheimeri*, the kind of ratsnake named after the naturalist and botanist Ferdinand Lindheimer. In those days, its common name was Texas Ratsnake. Whew, that's a lot to keep up with! I don't use scientific names very much in this book, because I want to focus on how these animals live, and the common or English name will work well enough for that. There is plenty of time for you to learn scientific names later, if you want to.

What's Next in This Book?

Right now, you may or may not be that interested in the science of herpetology. You may be drawn to reptiles and amphibians because they are fascinating and beautiful, and you might really enjoy seeing them in the wild or holding a particular animal. Being interested in them and enjoying watching them is just fine, whether you become a scientist or not. What I want to do in this book is to support your attraction to these animals by offering stories, descriptions, and facts about them, whether herpetology becomes a lifelong obsession for you or not.

In the next pages, we will look at some of the ways reptiles and amphibians have been important to us. These animals have been part of our cultures and religions, and they often appear in our books and movies. In later chapters we will talk about herps and how they live, by imagining a visit to several of the places they are found. Those places include a creek, the woods, rivers and bottomland forests, the desert, and the plains of the United States. Why focus on the United States? Lots of books include exotic animals like the pythons of Asia and Africa, or the chameleons of Madagascar. I want to emphasize how exciting our own native herps are and prepare you to get out and see these animals on your own field trips. I will pick several kinds of reptiles and amphibians in each place and discuss general facts about herps by telling each animal's story. In that way, we will cover how frogs begin life as tadpoles, how snakes move, how a turtle can pull its head into its shell, and a lot of other things. At the end, I'll talk about some of the skills that will help you search for and find herps. We will talk about when—and if—it is appropriate to catch one of them. Our discussion will also include the benefits of having someone guide you as you get out in the field looking for herps, and how to plan for outings.

How Can You Learn More?

Let's say you are one of those people who are burning to know more about herps, and you want to see some of our native species in the wild. I believe this book will be a useful guide for getting acquainted with these animals, but what else can you do? There are several ways to learn and get more experience.

A Strecker's Chorus Frog (photo by the author)

1. Join a herpetological society. There are many local herpetological societies or clubs around the United States, and visiting or becoming a member can be a way to learn from informative talks and make friends who share your interest. Each society may have a different emphasis, such as keeping exotic herps as opposed to going out to see native species, or having activities for young people as opposed to adults. If there is a society that meets near you, it may be helpful to go as a visitor and check it out.

2. Visit nature centers and wildlife refuges and sign up for their programs. Not only can you learn a lot by becoming familiar with places herps and other animals live, but these places often have programs that let you see these animals close up or give you guided experience in the field. After my first experiences with snakes in Colorado, my family moved to Texas and got me involved with a local museum that had a wonderful natural history program. Several of us practically lived at the museum and became trusted helpers with the live animal displays, scientific collections, and field trips. You will be lucky if you find a program even a little bit as intense and wonderful as that one was!

3. Explore internet resources about herps. For example, the Society for the Study of Amphibians and Reptiles (SSAR)[3] maintains a website with lots of information, including a section with articles on how to become a herpetologist and other topics. Similarly, the Center for North American Herpetology website[4] has links to lots of information. If you use the citizen science app iNaturalist,[5] you can look at what kinds of plants and animals people are seeing in different places and add your own observations. As I'm sure you know, the internet is a place with few rules, so it is a good idea to look for reputable and trustworthy sources of information like museums, professional organizations, zoos, and so on. And of course, always remember that people you meet online are not always who they seem—be careful out there!

4. Find a mentor. This might be someone at the nature center or herpetological society who can guide you in practicing the skills you need. For example, if you want to catch and handle a few of the herps you find in the wild, it is very important to do it in a way that is safe for you and for the animal you catch. This book will help prepare you, but some skills are best learned through guided experience. I think the best mentors know the importance of fun and at the same time have good judgment. The words "extreme" and "just go for it" have no place in mentoring a young herpetologist. It is not a reality show, and injuries will not add to the fun of being in the field! Taking things one step at a time and being careful will allow you to enjoy the extreme moments that will come along. Getting good skills and being aware of what you're doing make it possible to "go for it" just enough to have fun.

5. Read more books. Occasionally there is a good program on TV, and there is really good information on the internet, assuming that you go to trustworthy sites. The information you get that way is often in small, easily digested packets. The value of books is that the best ones can stitch the small packets together into a bigger picture. Books can give you something closer to the whole story, and they can show how things are related to each other. The bibliography at the end of this book lists other books that tell even more of the "story" of the reptiles and amphibians of the United States.

CHAPTER 2

In Our Imaginations

Reptiles and amphibians have inspired many stories and tales. Sometimes we are attracted to the odd ones, the weird ones that seem so hard to understand. Often the dangerous ones or the truly big ones stick in our imaginations and become the monsters or heroes of our stories. The dinosaurs have played a starring role in many tales, maybe because many of them were huge or dangerous, or because we enjoy trying to imagine a time so long ago. Let's explore just a few of the ways that reptiles and amphibians have shaped the stories told by cultures around the world. While we're at it, we can talk about how the dinosaurs are related to modern herps.

Folk Tales, Cultural Beliefs, and Myths

Reptiles and amphibians have been important figures in how some groups of people have understood the world. For example, in a Chinese creation myth, the world is supported on the back of a giant, immortal tortoise. Its four legs are the four corners of the earth, and its rounded back not only supports the earth but represents the dome of the sky.[1] There are similar stories in India and Tibet, and in North America as well—the Sioux believed that the earth was a giant turtle floating on water. Such myths probably draw on the themes of the strength and long lives of turtles. Do not think that the people who told these stories took

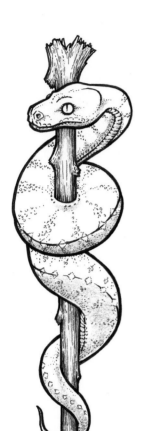

The Rod of Asclepius (illustration by Jack Jeansonne)

them literally, the way we might talk about a particular turtle we saw. Myths are ways of talking about bigger things than just a turtle floating on the water. Some Native American creation myths describe how the world came about through the generosity of everything that exists in nature. Each animal contributed its own unique gifts, and each part of nature, including humans, depended on the other. The story is not really about a specific turtle. It is about a way of living in the world, and what kinds of relationships we were born to have with the rest of nature.

In Aesop's fables, the persistence of turtles is illustrated in the tale of the Tortoise and the Hare. In it, the human qualities of humility and consistency (as shown in the plodding turtle) wind up being more important than the arrogance of the faster hare.

Snakes have appeared in the religion and mythology of people everywhere. In the biblical story of creation, the snake is portrayed as intelligent, devious, and able to speak, convincing Eve to eat the forbidden fruit of the Tree of Knowledge of Good and Evil. In Greek mythology, the god Asclepius was associated with healing and treating ailments. Asclepius wielded a rod with a snake twined around it, probably linked to the belief that he had been taught secret wisdom by a serpent. This "Rod of Asclepius" has been widely used to represent the healing arts and is part of the logo of many medical organizations.[2]

In Native American cultures, it was common to assign human

or even magical qualities to animals, and rattlesnakes appeared in many stories and ceremonies. One of those ceremonies is the Hopi Snake Dance, an annual tradition of the Hopi people of Arizona. In the arid region where the Hopi live, growing crops is difficult, and the Snake Dance is a sort of prayer for rain and crop fertility. The event takes place over nine days, beginning with the capturing of local snakes that may include harmless gopher snakes or racers but also the Prairie Rattlesnake.[3] In the initial days of the event, the captured snakes are kept in a kiva (an underground room) while prayers and rituals are performed. Among the items made by snake priests are "snake wands," short sticks with two eagle feathers. These wands are used to direct the snakes' movement or get them to straighten out when they coil defensively. On the final day, the snakes are washed and brought out of the kiva, and the snake priests dance while using their teeth and lips to hold the snakes by the neck. Afterward, the snakes are carried some distance away, to the north, south,

A Prairie Rattlesnake, one of the species used in the Hopi Snake Dance (photo by the author)

east, and west, and released. The snakes have been prepared as messengers to the gods, asking for rain and good crops.

Amphibians also appear in the mythology and tales of various cultures. In *The Book of the Toad*,[4] Robert DeGraaff describes a variation of the "Beauty and the Beast" story. As he returns from a journey, a man picks a rose for his youngest daughter. When he picks it, a headless man comes out of the ground and demands the father's life, or else his daughter must come and live forever at the house of the headless man. The story proceeds in a close parallel to "Beauty and the Beast," with the daughter taking her father's place and living as a sort of willing prisoner. Her daily companion is not the headless man, but a giant toad who takes care of the house and slips into her room by night as she sleeps. One night, she pretends to sleep but keeps her eyes open as the toad enters the room. Slipping out of his warty skin, he appears

Could there be a handsome young man under this toad's skin, as described in the variation of the "Beauty and the Beast" story? (photo by the author)

as a handsome young man. The girl grabs up the toad skin and destroys it, breaking a spell that a witch had cast upon the young man. This is one of many stories that seem to illustrate how ugliness may disguise underlying beauty, and how love may transform things for the better.

In our time, stories and folktales mostly take the form of movies and books. Herps have been the subjects of a great many movies, some of them silly and others more thought-provoking. Their appearance in some movies, like *Snakes on a Plane* and *Anaconda*, has little to offer except exaggeration of the danger snakes pose to humans. One movie blending the silly with just a little thoughtfulness is *Frogs*, which tells about a wealthy man and his family, living in a mansion on an island surrounded by swamp. It appears that the man has polluted much of the area with pesticides. Most of the movie is about the wildlife (including hordes of frogs) taking revenge against the humans who have poisoned their homes.

Among the books that feature reptiles and amphibians, one stands out vividly for me. It is *The Lost World*, by Sir Arthur Conan Doyle, who also wrote the Sherlock Holmes stories. In *The Lost World*, Professor Challenger claims to have traveled to a plateau in South America where dinosaurs still live. Responding to the disbelief and ridicule of others, he plans another expedition to bring back proof. A journalist, an adventurer, and another professor come along for the trip. Not only is this a story about encounters with dinosaurs, but there are unforgettable moments like their travel through a swamp and an attack by numerous Jararacas, a South American pit viper. This was surely the first time I ran across stories of "nests" of venomous snakes and people being chased by them. Later on, I would hear similar stories about the cottonmouth, one of our native venomous snakes. The stories are not true about either kind of snake. However, Sir Arthur Conan Doyle knew how to use fantasy and danger to tell a good story.

Dinosaurs and Other Prehistoric Creatures

Reptiles and amphibians have been on the earth for many millions of years, while we have walked the planet for only about 300,000 years.[5] Only in fairly recent times have we known how far back the herp family tree goes, or how amazing some of those prehistoric animals were. In the 1800s, our understanding of the various ages of prehistory increased a great deal, and we began to see that most species that we would recognize as kinds of animals have lived during three great eras: the Paleozoic, Mesozoic, and Cenozoic. Also during the 1800s, the term "paleontology" came into use. Paleontology is the science that tells the story of prehistoric life using fossils and other evidence. Another term came into use during that time—"dinosaur." That word, which literally means "terrible lizard," was coined by one of several British scientists[6] who first described fossil bones as belonging to these ancient reptiles. Since that time, dinosaurs have captured our imaginations. There are dinosaur skeletons in major museums, model dinosaurs for kids to play with, and life-size animatronic models that really seem to bring these ancient reptiles to life.

Amphibians and reptiles—or early relatives of these animals—got their start long before the time of the dinosaurs. For example, 270–280 million years ago, toward the end of the Paleozoic era, a compact, two-foot-long creature called *Seymouria* lived on land as an adult.[7] It seems to have had to return to water to lay eggs, which would have hatched into aquatic larvae in the same way that amphibians do. And during roughly that same period lived the sail-backed *Dimetrodon*, which is often mistaken for a dinosaur. It reached about eleven feet long, and a series of long spines growing from its vertebrae supported a big fin along its back. Not only was *Dimetrodon* not a dinosaur, but it was more closely related to the earliest mammals than to what we think of as reptiles.[8]

DRAGONS

Some people wonder whether the myths and legends about dragons started with earlier cultures finding dinosaur fossils. Huge dragons with scales and snake-like or lizard-like bodies appear in the stories people have told over most of the world. The long, serpentine dragons of China were often associated with rain, and people are said to have offered prayers or dances in attempts to get dragons to bring rain (compare this to the Hopi Snake Dance described in this chapter). Four-legged, winged, fire-breathing dragons appeared in stories and legends of the European Middle Ages. Such dragons were often depicted as very smart and very greedy, hoarding treasure in remote caves or other hiding places. One such beast who is familiar to modern readers is Smaug, the enormous dragon in J. R. R. Tolkien's *The Hobbit*. If Smaug is reptilian, then we might suppose that Bilbo Baggins (the hobbit hired by the dwarves to sneak into the dragon's lair) is actually a herper!

A dragon (illustration by Jack Jeansonne)

Are Modern Reptiles Descended from Dinosaurs?

Some of our modern reptiles remind us strongly of dinosaurs. Just watch a big monitor lizard, moving with the confident stride of a powerful predator. It is easy to imagine it prowling around a Mesozoic savanna among the dinosaurs. You may have seen the Australian Frilled Lizard, a fairly large reptile with a startling defensive display. When it is threatened, the folds of skin that are normally kept along its neck are brought forward like an umbrella suddenly opening, framing its gaping mouth and head and making it look much bigger and more threatening. This is such an amazing display that it inspired the creation of a medium-sized, frilled dinosaur in the movie *Jurassic Park*. There certainly seems to be a logical connection between the dinosaurs and some modern lizards. But how closely are they related?

In the reptile family tree, the lizard branch and the dinosaur branch split around the beginning of the Mesozoic (around 250 million years ago), with the earliest snakes splitting off from early lizards some time later.[9] No matter how much any modern lizards remind us of dinosaurs, they did not come from the "terrible lizards," regardless of the name. The turtles are also a separate lineage from the dinosaurs. Their branch of the family tree split off before the dinosaurs came along, and they have kept going all the way to the present with relatively few changes in their basic body structure. When I was about ten years old, I visited the Denver Museum of Nature & Science and stood in front of the massive skeleton of an extinct sea turtle and felt very small! The turtle goes by the scientific name *Protostega*, and it grew to as much as ten feet long. There are giant sea turtles still living, such as the Leatherback Sea Turtle, which may grow to six or seven feet long, but nothing as big as *Protostega*.

What about crocodilians—where is their branch of the reptile family tree? The alligator, crocodile, and other related reptiles fall within a group called the "archosaurs," which gave rise to the dinosaurs, modern crocodilians, and birds. This means that the

A skeleton of the prehistoric sea turtle *Protostega*, which captured
the author's imagination in visits in the early 1960s (Photo ©
Denver Museum of Nature & Science)

crocodilians are more closely related to dinosaurs than any other
living reptiles. If you visit our southern wetlands where alligators
or crocodiles live, you are as close as you will get to visiting
"Jurassic Park."

Modern and prehistoric, real and fanciful, reptiles and
amphibians have played a role in the stories we have told
throughout history. Because these animals can be powerful,
sometimes dangerous, and different from us in ways that
we struggle to understand, they have truly captured our
imaginations. Our next step will be to take a closer look at the
real herps that are alive today, to know what makes them what
they are and to understand how they live.

CHAPTER 3

At the Creek

Leopard Frogs, Watersnakes, and Snapping Turtles

Imagine you are at a creek somewhere. There are fish in the clear water, birds in the trees, and several species of herps in and around the water. We are going to focus on three of those herp species to see what we can learn about amphibians and reptiles in general.

From Tadpole to Frog

In a shallow part of one of the pools in the creek, a group of tadpoles is grazing on the algae that grows on rocks and other surfaces. Each one looks like an olive-green grape with a tail. When a heron steps into the water, they move their tails rapidly from side to side to push through the water and out of reach of the bird's sharp beak. About a month ago, these tadpoles were small, dark embryos in a cluster of about a thousand clear, jelly-like eggs. Once they grew for a few days and pushed out of the eggs, they were in some ways still embryos and in other ways they were animals that had to live in the world, find food, and escape from predators. Now they spend their days gorging on algae and growing, so that in another month they can transform

A creek where several species of herps might live (photo by the author)

into little Leopard Frogs. Their mouths have rough surfaces to scrape off the material they eat, and they pull water into their mouths, past internal gills to get oxygen, and out through a small opening or spiracle located behind the head and low on the side of the body.

The transformation they go through is amazing. The eyes gradually become bigger and positioned in the typical frog manner, like they're popping out of the head. The mouth, stomach, and intestines are remodeled from a small scraping disk to jaws with teeth and a tongue that can capture insects. Tadpoles go from eating plant or decaying material to eating "meat," if you think of crickets and earthworms as meat. The tails shrink and the back legs grow from little "buds" at the back of the body. Toward the end of the process, as the back legs grow big enough to be useful, the front legs emerge. They develop under the skin and then "pop out" of the tadpole's body. At this point, the gill-breathing aquatic tadpole is about ready to be an air-breathing land-dwelling frog. The word for all these changes is *metamorphosis*, meaning a change from one form to another.

The days pass, and many of the tadpoles are eaten by predators. Some wander into deeper water and are consumed by sunfish that detect their movement and dart over and suck them into their mouths. Some are picked off by watersnakes cruising through the shallows, picking up their scent in the water and watching for movement as the tadpoles shift to a new patch of algae. Mother frogs lay an incredible number of eggs because many tadpoles will be eaten by other animals. Those big numbers ensure that some of the tadpoles will make it to adulthood.

Now, three months after this clutch of eggs was laid, one of those tadpoles is a young Leopard Frog. The bright, bulging eyes have oval-shaped pupils. A Leopard Frog can see well close up and can see color as well. Its vision is particularly sensitive to movement. A cricket might sit still in front of this frog without

A Southern Leopard Frog (photo by the author)

anything happening, but as soon as it started moving, it would register in the frog's vision and be eaten.

This particular day, what those Leopard Frog eyes see is two humans walking along the creek. The boy and girl follow the water's edge and they are coming very close. The frog leaps from the bank into the water, swimming a short distance to a clump of aquatic plants and scrunching under their cover and out of view of the kids. As the boy and girl search the water near where the frog jumped in, it remains motionless. The eyes that detected the danger are protected by a fairly clear extra eyelid that closes from the bottom, called the nictitating membrane. Through it, the frog can still see its surroundings underwater.

After several minutes with no disturbance in the water and no huge shadows passing nearby, it seems the danger has passed. Our Leopard Frog swims closer to the shore and floats at the surface, with its bulbous eyes and part of its snout above water. There is no danger, and it will soon swim to the bank and hop under some overhanging reeds. Soon, a spider skitters along the ground nearby. The spider, unaware of the nearby frog, walks right in front of it. In a motion too quick to follow, the frog eats it.

What happened to the spider is this: the Leopard Frog's mouth opened and its tongue flipped over to land on the spider. The tongue of a frog or toad is attached at the front of the mouth, not the back, so that the tongue flips upside down, landing on whatever is in front of the frog. Since the tongue is sticky, the spider was carried back into the frog's mouth when the tongue returned. Then the mouth closed and the eyes pushed downward, bulging into the roof of the frog's mouth, pushing the spider down and into the esophagus. One spider, down the hatch!

There are four kinds of Leopard Frogs in the United States: the Northern, Southern, Plains, and Rio Grande Leopard Frogs. All of them are medium sized, roughly three or four inches in length, with large back legs and webbed toes. From the eye down the back on each side is a ridge of skin called the *dorsolateral ridge*, and there are spots scattered over the body. Leopard Frogs are generally found around creeks, ponds, marshes, and other wetlands, although they sometimes wander a little distance from the water. They have damp, slightly slimy skin and are at risk of drying out and dying if they stray too far from moisture. They tend to be active at night, another strategy to minimize overheating and drying.

A Watersnake and Her Babies

Late on a spring afternoon, the sun glints off a ripple in the water where a snake has slipped below the surface. She is hunting, and since she found no frogs around the edge of this pool in the creek, it's time to search underwater. Her long body is the color of cocoa, with a hint of a pattern of dark blotches down her back. As a baby she was brightly marked, with dark rounded blotches on her back and dark bars alternating with a pinkish color on her sides. That pattern slowly faded as she grew, and a plain chocolate brown almost replaced it. Plain-bellied Watersnakes like this one start out with bold patterns and gradually become rather plain colored above, with yellow belly scales below—or in some parts of the country their belly scales are orange or red orange.

She swims along the bottom, hugging the edges of rocks and poking into every hiding place where a tadpole might be resting. She flicks the tips of her forked tongue frequently, testing the water and rocks for the scent of fish or frogs. Along the edge of a larger rock she detects the scent of fish more strongly, and she becomes more alert, moving faster and tongue-flicking more rapidly. The watersnake finds a pocket where the overhanging rock forms a small cave, and there a sunfish is hiding. The snake's snout slowly moves toward the fish, and then with a lightning-quick move, she grabs it and begins to swallow. Her little teeth are sharp and angled toward the back of her mouth so that while a fish or frog can move toward her throat, the teeth keep it from getting away. While one side of her head grips the fish tightly, the other side stretches forward to get a new grip on the fish and pull it in. Then the other side takes a turn stretching farther over the fish, continuing the process of swallowing.

SNAKE TONGUES AND THE SENSE OF SMELL

Snakes are famous for having slender, forked tongues that they can extend, wave up and down, and pull back into their mouths. Many people don't know that the purpose of all that tongue-flicking is to pick up chemical cues and bring them into the mouth, where they can be sensed by the snake's vomeronasal organ, otherwise known as the Jacobson's organ. It is located just above the roof of the snake's mouth. It is an important part of the sensory system of various herps, but it is really well developed in snakes (and some lizards). The snake's tongue does not taste or detect odors by itself; what it does is bring chemical cues into the mouth, where those cues stimulate the vomeronasal organ. Snakes can also smell in the ordinary way when they breathe scents into the nose.

A Great Plains Ratsnake with its tongue extended
(photo by the author)

After swallowing the sunfish, the watersnake heads for the shore. She swims in a slow, leisurely way, her body bending side to side in S curves that push against rocks along the bottom. As she crosses a deeper part of the creek, those curves push against the water and she moves forward gracefully. Pulling out onto the shore, the snake's body finds all kinds of irregularities to push against—rocks, plant stems, and uneven places in the soil. The outer part of each curve of her body presses against these things, and as she travels forward that muscle contraction moves down her body, pressing against that same spot until she has passed it. To a person who is watching, it may look like a magic trick seeing a snake pour over rocks and branches like water moving of its own accord.

The next day, as this watersnake is basking on a branch over the water, she is approached by a male of the same species. His pattern and color are just like hers, but he is considerably smaller and more slender; as with several other species of snakes,

A Plain-bellied Watersnake from Texas (photo by Viviana Ricardez)

watersnake females grow larger than males. This male has tracked her by using his tongue to pick up chemical traces along her path. He approaches and tongue-flicks all along her back, while she remains still on the branch. After a short time, she drops into the water and he follows, swimming just alongside or behind her. She leaves the water and stops in an area with some fallen branches and dappled shade from the leaves of plants growing in the damp creek bank. The male watersnake rubs his chin along her back, with his body draped along hers and seeming to twitch or jerk regularly. After several minutes of this, his cloaca aligns with hers. The cloaca is a sort of general-purpose opening to the body where wastes are expelled, eggs are laid (or babies born), and mating takes place. From the base of his tail, one of the male's two hemipenes is everted into her cloaca. Hemipenes are paired copulatory organs (one on each side) ordinarily kept inside the base of the tail. When used, a hemipenis expands like a balloon that was turned inside out but is now filling with fluid and turning the inside parts outside. After fertilization occurs, the hemipenis is retracted into the base of the male's tail.[1]

After mating takes place, the two snakes go their separate ways and may not see each other again. The female continues hunting and soon picks up the scent of an American Bullfrog. As she searches, she sees a young bullfrog jump toward the water. Lucky for her it is a young one, because a fully grown one would be too big for her to eat. Plain-bellied Watersnakes have a "sweet tooth" for frogs, compared to other kinds of watersnakes. Prey items eaten by Plain-bellied Watersnakes include several species of toads, treefrogs, and "true" frogs such as bullfrogs and Leopard Frogs.[2]

About three months have now passed, and this watersnake is heavy with babies. Her species is ordinarily fairly heavy bodied, but the back half of her body is swollen and more rounded than usual, because she is carrying thirteen baby watersnakes. As with other North American watersnakes, the babies will be born rather than hatched from eggs. While most reptiles lay eggs, a few lizards and some snakes give live birth.

On this hot August day, she rests in the shade while feeling contractions within her body. She raises her tail as her body passes the first of the babies, enclosed in a clear membrane. The little snake is brightly blotched, just as its mother was in her infancy. In a short time, the baby watersnake pushes against the membrane until it is able to push its snout through and take its first few breaths. Then it pushes the rest of the way through, leaving behind a lump of birth membranes and carrying a little umbilical scar, a sort of "belly button" about two-thirds of the way down its belly that will later disappear.

Another baby is born and soon pokes through its membranes. Every few minutes the mother watersnake gives birth to another tiny snake, each one about ten inches long. The babies are well nourished and do not need to eat immediately. Within a few days they will be hunting tadpoles and Cricket Frogs and may be lucky enough to find trapped minnows in drying pools of the creek. While we are learning a lot about maternal care in some snake species such as rattlesnakes, these baby watersnakes appear to be on their own from their first days of life.

Many kinds of watersnakes live in the United States, such as the Brown Watersnake, the Banded Watersnake, and about seven more species, including the Plain-bellied Watersnake. They are all harmless, even though they are not particularly friendly if they are picked up, because they become frightened and defensive.

An Ancient Predator: The Snapping Turtle

In one of the pools of the creek, something stirs within the mud and fallen leaves at the bottom. What looked a little like a dark gray rock begins to rise, and there are two greenish-olive eyes to the side of it, their pattern partly disguised by dashes and speckles of dark color. Below the snout are hard, pale jaws looking a little bit, from the front, like a grin. It is the head of a Snapping Turtle (until recently called the "Common Snapping Turtle"), rising toward the surface on a long, stout neck. Below, the broad shell is half hidden in leaves and mud. The turtle's neck is long enough for the nostrils to break the surface and get a breath of air without the turtle needing to swim up to the surface. And then that neck, speckled with bumps and fleshy projections and as big around as someone's wrist, pulls the head back down to the bottom, where it once again looks like a stone. The Snapping Turtle is very patient. While he is capable of chasing down prey, ambush hunting suits him pretty well, and at the moment this hunting style is about to pay off. A crayfish is making its way along the bottom of this pool. It walks along the bottom, past the Snapping Turtle's head, and stops about a foot in front of those vaguely grinning jaws. In a sudden, powerful movement, the turtle's head shoots forward and his jaws open. His throat expands, sucking water in and at the last second helping pull the crayfish within his jaws, which crunch through the hard shell of the crustacean. The jaws hold this meal in a strong grip until it is clear that the crayfish will not move, and then after another couple of crunches, it is swallowed. The turtle

A Snapping Turtle, just after being moved off a road by the author (photo by the author)

settles in to wait for another a fish to stray too close, or a tadpole to wiggle by, or even a young turtle to swim near. Snapping Turtles are not particular about food. They will scavenge the body of something that has died, and around a third of their diet may be leaves, fruit, algae, and other plant material.[3]

While they stay in the water a great deal, they sometimes travel on land and get killed or injured crossing roads. Trouble with people is more likely to happen when the turtle is out of the water, moving from place to place. Like any other reptile, a Snapping Turtle would rather avoid trouble and be left alone, but if you walk up to one it will probably think it is being attacked. The snapper may raise the back part of its body, while the front part stays low, and it will probably tilt its shell toward you like a shield. All this time, its head is pulled back to the front edge of the shell and its mouth is usually open, ready to lash out on that long neck and snap whatever is within reach. Its jaws close with quite a bit of power, and they are hard and sharp, capable of biting into a hand or an arm and tearing flesh. A turtle researcher friend showed me a video clip of his assistant handling a Snapping Turtle and getting bitten on the thigh.[4] The turtle briefly held on and then released. The bite quite obviously hurt; it cut into the leg and there was some bleeding, but no serious injury resulted. Although you need not be afraid of them, if you come across one of these turtles you should leave it alone. The combination of its long neck, lightning-fast speed, and strong jaws means that you might be hurt if you try to pick it up or tease it. A Snapping Turtle on the road can be helped across by nudging or pushing it with something like a broom. Trained and experienced people will handle such a turtle by the back edge of the upper shell (the carapace) or the back legs. They will not pick up a large Snapping Turtle by the tail, as that may injure its spine.

The Snapping Turtle looks a little prehistoric with its big body; strong, heavily clawed legs; and long tail. The truth is that all turtles are part of an ancient line of reptiles that has kept the same general body plan since the time of the earliest dinosaurs. The upper shell—the carapace—is made up of fused backbone,

HOW THE TURTLE HIDES ITS HEAD

How does a turtle pull its head inside its shell? The turtle's neck is not an accordion; it won't fold and collapse that way. Its head is connected to its body by neck bones, so how do those bones bend to bring the head within the shell? Turtles around the world have worked out two ways of doing this. One group bends the neck to the side, but none of those live in the United States. The other group, including all of our turtles, bends the neck downward in an S curve, pulling the head back under the shell. The backbone is fused with the rest of the upper shell up to about where the shoulders are, and there it drops down and becomes the neck. When the head is pulled in, one end of the neck bends down until it points back toward the tail, and the rest of the neck bends in the other direction, going forward and connecting to the skull. To extend its head forward, the turtle simply straightens the neck bones out, pushing its head forward.

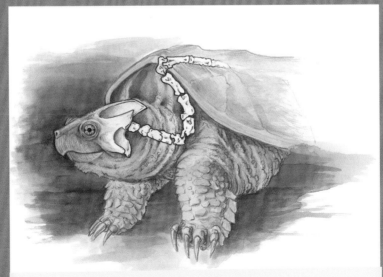

A Snapping Turtle, showing how neck vertebrae bend in an S shape when the turtle pulls its head within the shell (illustration by Jack Jeansonne)

ribs, and other bones, and the lower shell, called the plastron, is like a highly modified breastbone. Now think about your shoulder, with your collarbones, shoulder blades, and the socket where your arms attach. All of those are outside your ribcage, but the corresponding parts of a turtle are within the shell, meaning that they are inside its "ribcage." Somewhere during its evolutionary path, the turtle's skeleton was pretty seriously rearranged.

This particular Snapping Turtle is ancient in another way. He has lived in this creek for thirty years, which is old for a Snapping Turtle. Sometime in the late 1980s he hatched from an egg that was round and white just like the other nineteen eggs his mother laid that year. As a hatchling, he stayed mostly in shallow parts of the creek, hiding from the world as he ate and grew. A baby turtle's world is full of dangers, like the egret that stood tall in the water on its long legs, with white feathers ruffled in the breeze and a long bill ready to spear any small animal that moved. At night raccoons prowled the water's edge, looking for crayfish or frogs—but a little turtle would taste just fine, too. Sometimes raccoons dig up turtle nests and feast on the eggs. Really, it is amazing that this snapper or any of his brothers or sisters survived, but this one made it to adulthood.

Once they are adults, Snapping Turtles have few enemies that can get past the hard shell and sharp jaws. That is the basic plan that many turtles follow: keep laying eggs and live a long life, because most of the eggs and babies will be eaten. Only by surviving over a long lifetime will the snapper produce enough babies to keep its population going. It doesn't take the loss of very many adults run over on the road or hunted and eaten by humans before the Snapping Turtle population begins to decrease, and over the years they may disappear from a place.

There is an even bigger snapper than the one we talked about here. The Alligator Snapping Turtle is the biggest freshwater turtle in the United States, with wild specimens weighing as much as 150 pounds or more.[5] They are legally protected in most states, because hunting or collecting them is reducing their numbers.

CHAPTER **4**

In the Woods

Western Ratsnakes, Gray Treefrogs, and Texas Spiny Lizards

This time, picture yourself in an oak woodland, a place where sunlight filters down through oak leaves to shrubs and vines and then sandy soil covered with last year's fallen leaves. Rain gathers in little ponds here and there, and grasses grow in open areas. We will take a look at three more herp species that live here and see what they can teach us about reptiles and amphibians.

Climbing with No Hands

Among the oak leaves, there is a slight movement. Along a branch, something that looks a little like a second branch moves steadily toward the tree trunk. Its colors—gray, charcoal with flecks of white, and a little bit of lighter yellowish—are similar to the dark gray shades of the oak bark. Unlike a branch, it is moving, and at the forward end there is a slate-gray head from which a red tongue regularly flicks out to pick up cues from the surface of the bark. The snake's body is lined up along the branch, with an occasional kink that grips a rough spot or twig and pushes the snake forward. As this Western Ratsnake's head

An oak woodland in Texas (photo by the author)

nears the trunk, he inclines his neck and stretches up toward where the next branch grows from the trunk. As his head passes the next branch, he shifts to the side just slightly to hook a curve of his neck over the branch. The snake's body continues to move smoothly upward. What was a curve of his neck becomes a curve of his body and then a curve of his tail, pushing against that same branch as his body moves. He continues to grab irregular places in the bark and other branches, seeming to flow up the tree in one slow but steady movement. One reason the ratsnake is such a talented climber is its body shape. While the snake is rounded on the top, its sides tend to come straight down so that they meet the belly at right angles, in the same way a loaf of bread is rounded at the top and square at the bottom. The edges of the flat belly scales easily catch against irregularities and keep the snake from slipping back.

At the next branch, the scent molecules picked up by the ratsnake's tongue suggest that a bird is nearby, and he sees movement. The sparrow is preening its feathers, and the

A Western Ratsnake (photo by the author)

movement catches the ratsnake's attention. He is probably seeing the sparrow in shades of gray, as snakes may have pretty good vision for detail and movement, but it does not appear that they see in color. Like the eyes of most animals with backbones, reptile eyes have a pupil that adjusts the amount of light coming in, a lens to focus the image, and a retina to convert the image to signals that can be sent to the brain. Snake retinas have both rods and cones, but the cones, which are normally associated with color vision, do not have the different visual pigments needed for color vision.[1]

The ratsnake edges slowly forward, his head held back and his neck forming loops that will enable him to strike at his prey. He tongue-flicks again, picking up the scent of bird in the air. However, the bird (whose vision is keener than his) sees the movement of his tongue and immediately flies away. The

HOW SNAKES MOVE

One of the biggest challenges of life with no legs is moving from place to place. Snakes have to escape from enemies, hunt food (sometimes chasing it down), and find shelter, mates, and water. Different kinds of snakes live successfully on the ground, in trees, on desert sands, in wetlands, and even in the sea! As a result, they have developed several ways of moving through their environments:*

Lateral undulation—This is the familiar S curve movement in which the snake sends waves of contractions down the sides of the body, pushing loops of the body to the side and backward against things like stones or branches. This moves the body forward. A snake swims using lateral undulation, with curves of the body pushing against the water.

Rectilinear movement—In this pattern of movement, the snake slowly moves forward in something close to a straight line. At multiple points along the snake's belly, some muscles pull the belly scales upward and forward, while other muscles anchor the body and pull the rest of it forward. It looks a little like a caterpillar in motion, with alternating places on the belly stretching forward and then seeming to push backward. It is most commonly used by larger, heavy-bodied snakes such as pit vipers.

Concertina movement—A snake may climb a smooth tree trunk or move through a rodent burrow by anchoring the back part of the body (for example, bunching it up and pushing against the sides of a tunnel) while extending the front part forward. Then the front part of the body anchors itself in the same way while the rear part relaxes and is pulled forward.

Slide-pushing—On a smooth surface, the snake uses what looks like lateral undulation, but waves of movement travel down the body much faster than the snake travels. With little to push against, the snake slides forward only because of the friction between the belly and the surface.

Sidewinding—On sand dunes, pushing the body to the sides and backward might just move the sand around. Instead, some snakes lift a section of the body off the ground and move it forward and to the side, where it comes down and contacts the sand. By pushing downward, the body does not slip in the sand as much. The snake's body travels mostly sideways and leaves a series of disconnected J-shaped tracks in the sand.

snake sits for a moment, taking in his disappointment, and begins to crawl away. Ratsnakes such as this one must come up "empty-handed" several times for each bird they catch. Their greatest success in bird eating comes in nesting season, when they find nests of young birds not yet able to fly away.

Could the ratsnake have heard the bird? Maybe he would have known it was there more quickly if he had heard it calling. Some people mistakenly believe that snakes are deaf because they have no ears, at least on the outside. They have no eardrum or middle ear, but a small bone attached to the quadrate (a bone connecting the lower jaw to the rest of the head) connects to the skull so that it can transmit sound vibrations from the jaw to the inner ear.[2] They respond best to low-frequency sounds—from about 200 to 500 hertz, which includes a variety of sounds, as well as a lot of human speech—but snake hearing sensitivity drops quite a bit at higher frequencies or pitches. Snakes are not particularly good at getting airborne sounds to their inner ears, and it is thought that hearing as we think about it is not very important in the daily lives of snakes.

Birds are only one item on the ratsnake's menu, and the most frequent meals eaten are mice and rats, not birds.[3] After sunset on this same day, the Western Ratsnake is on the ground, moving along the edge of the woodland through tall native grasses. He picks up the scent of a cotton rat along a rodent runway, a little path through the grasses used by rodents. Following the scent along the runway, the snake comes upon a cotton rat loping toward him. The ratsnake immediately strikes at the rat, biting it at about the shoulder. The rest of the snake's body immediately wraps around the rat, throwing it off balance and keeping it from moving. Those reptilian coils are very strong, and they tighten so that the rat cannot breathe. If the rat exhales, the coils tighten further, so it cannot take a breath. Many people believe that the constriction snakes use kills their prey by suffocation, but death comes more quickly than that. The pressure on the rat's

A somewhat darker Western Ratsnake, though you can still see blotches down its back if you look closely (photo by the author)

body prevents blood from circulating, and it dies very quickly because its heart and blood vessels cannot work.

Sensing no struggle and no heartbeat, the ratsnake relaxes its hold on the rat and begins methodically exploring the rat's body and tongue-flicking almost continually. Finding the rat's nose, the snake opens his mouth and begins to swallow. Why does he start with the rat's head? Like other snakes, this ratsnake cannot bite off and chew pieces of what he eats. His only option is to swallow it whole. The rat's hair lies down easily from front to back, and its legs fold easily in that direction, too. If you are going to swallow something much bigger than your head, it helps if the parts of the meal fold back out of the way!

The Western Ratsnake is one of three kinds of large ratsnakes in the United States. The others are the Eastern and Gray Ratsnakes. The ratsnake genus also includes several other snakes in the United States, such as the Red Cornsnake, Great Plains Ratsnake, Eastern Foxsnake, and others.

A Frog with a Birdlike Voice

In these same woods, a couple of months earlier when spring brought a few warm days, a small frog grew restless in his shelter in a decaying log. He moved into the sunlight and warmed enough to move around. It had rained the night before, filling a low spot with shallow water. The frog hopped to the trunk of a small tree nearby, finding a place partly concealed by an overhanging branch. The air temperature was about 52°F, which feels cold to most of us, but with the sun on his back and a little shelter provided by the tree, this Gray Treefrog was not complaining.

Amphibians are "cold-blooded," like reptiles. This doesn't mean they have icy blood flowing through their veins—that is, unless they're sitting in an icy cold spot. What it means is that they don't generate body heat like we do. If an amphibian is basking in warm sunshine, it will absorb heat and be warm. If it is sitting in a patch of snow on a cold spring morning, it will be cold and will move somewhere a little warmer. Amphibians—and reptiles too—catch food, escape predators, and do other things only within a certain range of temperatures. If they're too cold their actions slow down, and below a certain point they may die. If they get too hot their bodies do not work right, and above a critical maximum temperature they will die.

An amphibian or reptile can tell whether its temperature is hot or cold because a part of its brain, the hypothalamus, can sense it. The hypothalamus is one of those lower parts of the brain that keeps body processes working right—the "regulating" brain rather than the "thinking" brain. It is sort of like a thermostat that decides what is the right temperature and senses whether the animal's body is too hot or cold. Being cold-blooded means that there is no heater in the body that

A Gray Treefrog (photo by the author)

the thermostat can turn on or off. Instead, the brain tells the animal to do something like move to a different place. That's how herps stay within the right temperature range. They shift into a warmer spot or position themselves in the sun, or they get under cover or sit in water to cool off.

Our treefrog spent a day or two eating small insects and basking when the sun appeared from behind the clouds during the day. At night, the clouds kept temperatures from falling below freezing, until one night when a cold front arrived. It was as if winter had returned, and the treefrog was exposed to temperatures below freezing. This would kill most species of reptiles and amphibians.

The Gray Treefrog survived the cold snap. Freezing kills when ice crystals form within the body, but some frogs (and perhaps some salamanders as well) can quickly convert stored glycogen into glucose, at concentrations that may be sixty times normal levels.[4] This prevents ice crystals from forming within the cells. Ice does form in the fluids outside the cells, and the frog appears to be frozen, but the high concentration of glucose acts like antifreeze within the cells and the frog does not die. The frog species known to be able to tolerate freezing—the Western Chorus Frog, Spring Peeper, Gray Treefrog, and Wood Frog—often spend the winter under leaves and other cover that may not always protect them from subfreezing temperatures. They also tend to breed early in the spring, when cold fronts can arrive and bring a brief return to freezing weather.

A few days later, clouds came streaming up from the south, dropping a half inch of rain and filling the shallow pool with water that was several degrees warmer. After dark, the treefrog was drawn to the edges of this pool, and he was joined by others with the same mottled pattern of lighter and darker gray color. One of them began to call, his throat expanding like a balloon and making a high, melodious sound. It was a trill, a little like a fast, stuttering string of chirps lasting two or three seconds. Then he was joined by another Gray Treefrog, making the same sound. A visitor in these woods might think some bird was calling in the darkness, but these were male treefrogs, calling to females of their species who were ready to lay eggs in the water. Soon, a chorus of dozens of Gray Treefrogs could be heard for a considerable distance, advertising their presence to females who would come to the pool to breed.

How do frogs and toads make these sounds? Most of them have vocal cords, and air is forced through them and into a vocal sac that helps broadcast the sound. In toads and most frogs, this sac expands under the throat like a balloon; in some frogs there are paired vocal sacs to either side of the jaw. Each species has its own call, despite the widespread idea that frogs and toads only croak or make "ribbit" sounds. Toad calls are often drawn-out trills—and some of them have been compared to the bleating of sheep or the turning of a wooden ratchet. On a spring night at a pond, sometimes you can hear several frog species calling. There can be the ongoing "grick-grick-grick" calls of Cricket Frogs, the honking or quacking sounds of Green Treefrogs, the low, banjo-like "gunk" of the Green Frog, and so on. It is hard to describe just how enchanting such a night can be, hearing a chorus of these calls in the darkness. The great herpetologist Archie Carr said, "Frogs do for the night what birds do for the day: They give it a voice." Up close, that voice can be loud; some louder species can produce sounds between 90 and 120 decibels,[5] which is comparable to the loudness of a car horn. Male frogs and toads use a great deal of energy in breeding calls, but the survival of the population depends on their calls reaching females who are ready to lay eggs. A wonderful book and CD set with photos, information, and audio recordings of calls is *The Frogs and Toads of North America*, by Lang Elliott and others.[6]

Frogs and toads can hear fairly well. They have eardrums that can be seen as circular patches on either side of the head. Behind them is a middle ear cavity with small bones that conduct sound back to the inner ear. A major purpose of hearing in frogs and toads is to detect calls from members of their own species during breeding activities.

There is a second kind of Gray Treefrog, and it is hard to tell the two apart except by looking at their chromosomes (the genetic material in their cells) or listening to their calls. The call of the Cope's Gray Treefrog is not as musical as that of the Gray Treefrog in the story above. A number of other kinds of treefrogs are found in the United States, including the Green Treefrog, the Squirrel Treefrog, the Bird-voiced Treefrog (which also has a high, chirping call), and others. These frogs are all relatively small and have flattened toe pads that allow them to stick to smooth surfaces like a leaf—or a window.

The Tale of the Lizard's Lost Tail

Later in the spring, as the sun warmed the woods, a Texas Spiny Lizard spent her days clinging to sunny patches on tree trunks and eating lots of the spiders, flies, grasshoppers, and caterpillars she found. Perched three or four feet up the tree and facing down toward the ground, the lizard could spot a grasshopper among the grasses, dash down and grab it, and climb back up the trunk to eat it. As she waited in ambush with her tail curled slightly over her body, she hung from the bark by her sharp little claws and watched not only for meals but for things that might eat her. The approach of a bird like a Mississippi Kite could mean death, and she was capable of going from perfectly still to a fast run in an instant. "Running" might take her farther up the tree or around to the other side, out of sight, and those sharp claws would allow her to go as fast on a vertical tree trunk as she could on the ground.

A Texas Spiny Lizard (photo by the author)

While she stayed perfectly still on the tree trunk, her camouflage made her hard to find. Each row of scales of her back overlapped the ones behind, like shingles. Each of those scales was raised and pointed at the end, making her look spiny, as the name suggests. Those scales were mostly gray to grayish brown, with an irregular pattern of black squiggles, wavy black bars running across her back, and a band of light gray at each side. Where her tail began, the scales had a cinnamon background color as if she had been dipped in rust. She looked just like a patch of oak bark, unless you looked closely. This strategy, called crypsis, allowed her to avoid being found and eaten. Through colors that matched the branches or tree trunks, with spiny scales that made it harder to see her exact outline, and by the habit of sitting perfectly still, she might keep from being found by a predator.

No matter how fast or how well camouflaged, no lizard can avoid predators all the time. One additional trick many lizards have is that their tails can break off if a predator (like a skunk, snake, or bird) grabs it. One afternoon, when she was on the ground between her usual tree hangouts, a crow spotted her movement. The bird dropped quickly, but the spiny lizard was a little too fast. The crow grabbed the lizard's tail, which broke where the crow grabbed it. The lizard kept running to the nearest tree and scampered up a short distance, on the far side where she would not be seen. Meanwhile, the tail twisted in the bird's beak as if it were alive, keeping the crow focused on the tail while the lizard got away.

Later that day, a male Texas Spiny Lizard watched as another male climbed a nearby tree. He seemed to stand up taller at the sight of this invader, and then he did several "pushups," flexing his forelegs to drop and then push up rapidly. This was an attempt to show this new lizard who was in charge of this territory, as if to say, "These trees are mine—go somewhere else." The other male remained motionless. More pushups followed, and the new lizard turned and scampered to the ground. He would move a little way off to try to find a tree unclaimed by a dominant male spiny lizard. When he found it, he would claim

THE PROS AND CONS OF LOSING A TAIL

Losing your tail is clearly better than losing your life. Many lizards can lose their tails quite easily when grabbed, and a few even help things along by contracting muscles that allow the tail to be released. There is little bleeding and the stump heals quickly. Later, the lizard grows a new tail, though it may be shorter or have different-looking scales. The lizard does not grow new bones in the tail, however, just a rod of cartilage. There are a few disadvantages to losing the tail. One is that the tail can store fat reserves, so a lost tail is lost energy. It is also possible that the lizard cannot run with the same balance and coordination. Additionally, a lizard that loses its tail may also lose some social status with nearby lizards of the same species and have a harder time defending a preferred territory. It is pretty likely that the lizard would say it's all worth it to escape being eaten by a predator!

that tree and would do his own pushup displays to show any other males that he was the dominant lizard in that place.

Lizard social interactions are mostly about dominance and defending territory, or else courtship. Most of the communication among lizards involves head-bobbing, pushups, or displaying a colorful "dewlap" under the throat, and each species finds its own specific way of using these signals. For example, when two similar species live in an area, each will use a particular pattern and rhythm of bobbing or pushing up, like a slightly different language that only lizards of the same species respond to. If all this seems like middle school drama, keep in mind that it helps ensure that the lizards have enough space for adequate food and shelter, and that healthier and stronger individuals pass their genes on to the next generation.

The Texas Spiny Lizard is one species within a large group or genus (*Sceloporus*). Other spiny lizards include bigger ones like the Crevice Spiny Lizard and smaller ones such as the prairie lizards and fence lizards. Generally these lizards have spiny-looking scales and a great ability to climb rocks and trees.

CHAPTER 5

In the Rivers and Bottomlands

Cottonmouths, Alligators, Red-eared Sliders, and Marbled Salamanders

Rivers and the areas around them are full of wonders. Where they flow through lowlands, they can create bottomland forests. In such forests, trees like cottonwood, elm, bald cypress, and oak grow tall. When there is a lot of rain, bottomlands get flooded, and many times there will be scattered, shallow ponds within the woods. Here are four of the many kinds of reptiles and amphibians you might see there.

Cottonmouth, or Water Moccasin?

In one of these bottomland forests, a dark, almost charcoal-colored snake makes his way among the fallen branches. His body is marked with broad wavy bands, but they are dark and not easily noticed. The snake pokes his snout into hidden pockets of leaves and soil under pieces of dead wood, searching for something to eat. This chunky snake is a Northern Cottonmouth, a venomous snake related to copperheads. Some people call it a "water moccasin," but regardless of which name you use, it is still the same snake.

The name "cottonmouth" comes from its reaction when threatened. Often it will tilt its head back and hold its mouth open, not attempting to bite but just displaying the pale whitish tissues inside its mouth. If the threat (an animal or a person) moves, the snake may shift its position to keep facing the intruder and gape its mouth even wider. It is hard to know what the snake is experiencing, but mouth-gaping does not mean that it is trying to bite or attack. The effect of this mouth-gaping might be to startle or warn an enemy and so keep either the snake or the other animal from being hurt. Is the snake mad? We need to be careful about guessing what the cottonmouth could be "thinking," but it is likely that the snake is afraid. Its mouth-gaping (while usually

A Northern Cottonmouth, defensively mouth-gaping—it is not attempting to bite (photo by the author)

FANGS AND VENOM

A snake's fangs, venom glands, and venom evolved from salivary glands and teeth. They are very specialized ways of catching prey, but they are also used in defense. The information below applies to snakes in the United States.

Fangs are enlarged teeth that are used to inject venom. Rattlesnakes, copperheads, and cottonmouths (pit vipers) as well as coralsnakes have hollow fangs that are like hypodermic needles. The fangs of pit vipers fold against the roof of the mouth when not in use. When a pit viper opens its mouth to strike at something, it rotates the fangs downward. With the mouth fully open, the fangs are pointed straight toward the target. The snake can control the movement of the fangs—if you watch a pit viper open its mouth to stretch its jaws, it may move each fang separately as it stretches. The fangs of coralsnakes are smaller and fixed in their position. These snakes always have several replacement fangs growing behind the ones currently in use. When they periodically shed fangs, new ones are ready for use. The enlarged teeth of rear-fanged snakes (such as the black-headed snakes) are not hollow and are usually grooved. Their mild venom flows down the groove and into the bitten animal.

Pit vipers and coralsnakes produce venom in glands along the upper jaws and sides of the head. Each gland is connected to a fang by a duct, and when the snake strikes, muscles can contract to force venom through the fangs. The snake can voluntarily control these muscles, so it can choose to inject a little venom, a lot, or none at all.

Snake venom contains a number of proteins and enzymes. Some break down muscle and connective tissue, destroying red blood cells and making blood vessels leak, as well as making it easier for the venom to penetrate the body. Other components of snake venom work on nerve transmission, with results such as paralysis or shutting down breathing. Most pit viper venom includes primarily the stuff that breaks down tissue, and such venom is described as "hemotoxic." It works to stop a prey animal in its tracks and begin the process of digestion from the inside. Coralsnake venom emphasizes interfering with the nervous system, and it is described as "neurotoxic."

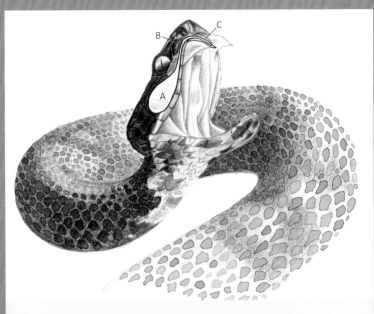

Pit viper venom apparatus. Venom is stored in a gland (A) and travels through a duct (B) through a hollow fang (C). (illustration by Jack Jeansonne)

shaking its tail vigorously) might be something like a "nervous habit" that is triggered when the snake is frightened.

The name "water moccasin" is harder to explain. In some parts of the country, both copperheads and cottonmouths have been called moccasins. People have sometimes called the ones that live in more upland areas (copperheads) "upland moccasins" to keep them separate from their cousins who live in swampy wetlands.

This snake is searching through the forest floor for a frog or maybe a watersnake to eat. Northern Cottonmouths are not particular about what's on the menu. They eat frogs, snakes, lizards, fish, mice, and other small animals. A cottonmouth might coil and wait to ambush a mouse, and in that case, it would bite the mouse and probably release it. As the venom disabled and killed the mouse, the snake would track it down and then eat it. Cottonmouths use a different strategy when they find frogs or fish, animals that are not affected as quickly by their venom. To keep a fish or frog from getting away, a cottonmouth will typically bite and hang on, and then swallow it.[1]

Our Northern Cottonmouth continues across the ground in this bottomland forest, under fallen branches and through leaf litter, without finding anything to eat. He reaches a shallow pool and does not hesitate to swim across it, gliding out into the dark water and using the curves of his body to push himself across the surface. Unlike the harmless watersnakes that usually swim underwater, the cottonmouth typically rides high in the water. This is not a hard-and-fast rule, but it is often true. Cottonmouths can swim underwater (and can bite and inject venom while submerged) but more often swim on the surface, thanks to a large lung that tends to make them float.[2]

A 'Gator in the Marsh

The cottonmouth wanders out of the forest and along the edge of a marsh. The trees give way to tall reeds growing out of mud and shallow water. The snake threads his way through the reeds and crosses some open water. His leisurely swim takes him near something in the middle of the water that looks like a knob of waterlogged wood with two eyes watching all around. A second knob, a few inches away, has two open nostrils breathing in. Then the nostrils close, clear membranes blink over the eyes, and the knobs begin to sink. Just visible in the dark water is the outline of a body, like a dark dragon with a muscular, saw-toothed tail.

This "dragon," actually an American Alligator, swims toward the water's edge and waits. Fifteen inches below the surface, he can watch the edge of the marsh with his eyes protected by nictitating membranes. Those membranes are like an extra set of clear eyelids, and their purpose is similar to that of goggles; they protect the eyes while letting the alligator see underwater. As he stays completely still among the reeds, a snake cruises along the surface of the water at the edge of the shore. It is the cottonmouth, continuing to hunt along the water's edge, unaware of the danger nearby. From underneath, all the alligator can see is belly scales, pushing forward a little and then bunching up in tight curves as the snake stops to rest. The alligator readies

A young American Alligator (photo by the author)

himself, and then with a sudden side-to-side movement of his tail he pushes himself forward as his jaws open and then close on the snake. After a couple of bites, the cottonmouth is dead. Moving his head upward, the 'gator tosses the snake's body to the back of his throat and swallows.

The alligator's sudden burst of speed is possible because of its big, muscular tail. It is rounded where it joins the body but gradually tapers and flattens so that it is tall and thin. When moved back and forth, it acts like an oar and pushes the 'gator forward. Although its legs seem small compared to its body, they are also powerful. On land, an alligator can run faster than we can for short distances. When we go walking and wading in and around marshes and rivers in the southeastern United States, we can be thankful that the American Alligator is usually shy and avoids contact with people, with a couple of exceptions. Females may defend nests, and any alligator might charge a person who gets too close. The most dangerous situation is created when people feed alligators.

An American Alligator swimming away from the shore (photo by the author)

Once they become accustomed to people and think of humans as sources of food, they are quite dangerous. As a result, a "nuisance" alligator may have to be trapped and killed. As one sign posted in alligator habitat put it, "A fed 'gator is a dead 'gator."

At twelve feet long, this alligator is a large one, but not abnormally large for a male. Female American Alligators do not get quite as large as males. He swims into deeper water, with slow side-to-side movements of his tail. His body is adapted in many ways for life in the water. The openings of an alligator's nostrils can close while underwater, and a flap at the back of the mouth keeps water from getting into the throat or breathing passages. Sensory organs in the skin around the face are triggered by pressure changes in the water, signaling the movement of a prey animal even if muddy water limits the 'gator's vision.[3] The ear openings can be closed when it is underwater.

These adaptations and the large size and strength of alligators make them top predators throughout the southeastern United States from North Carolina to Texas. They do well in coastal freshwater marshes and in wetlands along major river systems. That makes them very different from the American Crocodile, which is hanging on in South Florida, a threatened species being crowded out in many places because of habitat loss. Where alligators prefer freshwater and tolerate only a little salinity in coastal marshes, crocodiles are at home in brackish (somewhat salty) estuaries along the Florida coast. Crocodiles have a sort of olive-colored appearance and a narrow snout, with both upper and lower teeth (especially the fourth one) visible when the mouth is shut. The American Alligator is mostly black and has a broad, rounded snout. Its lower teeth cannot be seen when its mouth is shut, because the upper jaw overlaps it a little.

American Alligators were not always as common as they are today. In the 1950s and 1960s, commercial hunting and loss of habitat reduced their numbers to the point that in 1967 they were protected from hunting. They might have disappeared

A Red-eared Slider (photo by Viviana Ricardez)

altogether if they had not been declared endangered. American Alligator populations gradually returned to healthier numbers, and they became a real success story for the Endangered Species Act.

Basking in the Sun, Sliding into the Water

Twenty yards away from the drama between the alligator and cottonmouth, a turtle climbed up onto an exposed tree trunk and basked in the sunlight. The turtle noticed the alligator, turning her head a little toward where he was swimming, but she was not alarmed. If she swam near the 'gator, her hard, bony shell would not protect her from being eaten. But she was a good distance away and out of the water, so she had little need for fear.

This Red-eared Slider adjusted her position as the afternoon sun got a little lower in the sky. Her shell was fully exposed to the sunlight and she warmed herself a bit above the air temperature. She looked somewhat awkward as she rested on that wood sticking out of the water, like a dish balanced on a narrow shelf where it could easily fall off. That was actually part of the plan. Pond turtles such as the Red-eared Slider often bask in places where, if danger appears, they can give a slight push to slide into the safety of the water. Just a short distance down the marsh, five turtles were balanced on a log just above the water. A couple of Red-eared Sliders were joined by their cousins, two river cooters and a map turtle, all positioned on the log like plates carelessly stacked after washing. The map turtle was on top of one of the cooters, and the shells of the others overlapped each other, trying to get the best position in the sun. When a woman walked by on the nearby bank, bird-watching and not noticing the turtles, first one, then two, then all five of the turtles dropped into the water, where they evidently believed the bird-watcher was unlikely to follow.

The Red-eared Slider, named because of the patch of crimson on either side of the head behind the eye, was originally found from Texas to Mississippi and up to Kentucky, Illinois, Missouri, and parts of adjacent states. There are now scattered populations as far north as Michigan, as far east as New Jersey, and as far west as New Mexico. The delightful faces and beautiful green and yellow lines of the hatchling red-ears made them very popular in the pet trade, and they have been released or have escaped all over the world. This species is the world's most widespread freshwater turtle.[4] That is not a good thing, never mind that the Red-eared Slider is a wonderful turtle. When foreign turtles are introduced into an ecosystem in which they do not belong, they can outcompete some species of native turtles, bring new diseases, or otherwise throw things out of balance. Sometimes what seems like an act of kindness and freedom can result in serious problems.

The slider resting on the branch in the marsh, however, was part of a natural population of these turtles. But why did she climb out of the water to bask? Why not stay in the safety of the water all the time? One reason is that she can warm herself through direct exposure to sunlight. Drying out might reduce the number of leeches or other parasites on her skin. Still another reason is that she absorbs a particular part of the light spectrum, ultraviolet-B (UV-B), which is important for making vitamin D_3. That vitamin is needed for the formation of bones. Some animals get vitamin D_3 primarily through their diet, while others get much of it when sunlight hits their skin. Most turtles need regular exposure to sunlight to get enough vitamin D_3. In one experiment, captive Red-eared Sliders that were given supplemental UV-B exposure had much more vitamin D_3 in their blood than turtles that were not able to bask under UV-B lamps.[5]

Meanwhile, one of the sliders that dropped into the water is walking around at the bottom of the marsh. He swims to a new spot and then casually walks some more, nibbling on algae and looking for carrion or perhaps a water bug to eat. For an air-breathing reptile, he doesn't seem too concerned about

Texas River Cooters basking on the San Gabriel River (photo by the author)

coming up for air. Regularly, his jaw drops a little and then closes, as if he is chewing something. What he is really doing is pumping water across the lining of his mouth and throat, where some of the oxygen from the water transfers into his bloodstream.[6] This helps for a while, but soon the turtle needs to come to the surface for a breath of air.

In a few months, these turtles will face the beginning of winter. Since they do not generate their own body heat, how will they get through the days or weeks of freezing temperatures? The answer is that many of them will stay underwater, maybe dig into the mud at the bottom of the marsh and spend the winter there.

The Red-eared Slider has a couple of close relatives: the Yellow-bellied Slider, found from Mississippi east to Virginia, and the Cumberland Slider, found in a small area within Tennessee. Another group of similar turtles that live in rivers and other wetlands are called "cooters."

Late-Autumn Ponds and Marbled Salamanders

It is now November in the bottomlands. The leaves are falling and they form a deep, spongy carpet between the trees and around the fallen branches and rotting logs. The season is turning cold, and the forest is dotted with shallow pools, emptying into little streams that wind toward the marsh. Within the layers of leaves and fallen branches, a salamander becomes restless.

This salamander is the landlord of an abandoned burrow made some time ago by a White-footed Mouse. The mouse moved on, and the salamander discovered it and used it as a cozy place in which to ambush the spiders and earthworms that came along. Her chunky head, long body, and tail are black with irregular bands of silver gray across her back, identifying her as a Marbled Salamander. Her species and several related ones are known as "mole" salamanders. They are medium-sized amphibians that breathe with lungs and spend much of their time underground. Other species within

WINTER AT THE BOTTOM OF THE MARSH

Pond turtles have some pretty amazing ways of getting through the winter. To start with, they are pretty tolerant of cold temperatures. There are reports of them swimming in water as cold as 36°F, and on warm winter days they sometimes emerge to bask. However, they have to find shelter from freezing temperatures, and they often find it at the bottom of a pond or marsh. Here is how they and related turtles like map turtles and cooters survive:

> When underwater for a long period, some kinds of turtles can absorb enough oxygen through body tissues like the lining of the throat and the cloaca (the opening at the base of the tail into which the reproductive and digestive tracts empty). Other kinds of turtles don't get much oxygen that way but have worked out ways to keep their bodies working without oxygen.
>
> Diving to the bottom results in a dramatic decrease in the heart rate of Red-eared Sliders. The cold temperature drives the turtle's metabolism down, so that it needs little oxygen.
>
> In winter, submerged Red-eared Sliders survive mostly by their ability to tolerate anoxia (lack of oxygen) and to get what little energy they need primarily through anaerobic metabolism. That means that the cells are doing their work using chemical processes that don't require oxygen. While animals (and people) may use such processes during a quick burst of energy, we ordinarily could not keep it up. Because most activity of the hibernating turtle is shut down or greatly slowed, and the turtle has some remarkable body processes, it can stay submerged for a long time.

this group include the Tiger Salamanders, Ringed, Spotted, and Small-mouthed Salamanders, and others as well. They are found across many states of the United States and into Canada. Even though they have lungs, oxygen and carbon dioxide cross their skin pretty easily, and some of their respiration happens through the skin.

The cold temperatures from the approaching winter are no problem for this salamander. The mole salamanders may prefer temperatures between about 34 and 80°F, and another group, the lungless salamanders, may prefer temperatures between freezing and just under 80°F.[7] Because they spend much of their lives belowground or under logs and leaf litter, these salamanders usually avoid extremely hot summer temperatures and winter freezes. They cruise through burrows and under leaf litter, deeper underground when it is hot but sometimes moving around on the surface after rains.

This salamander is restless because it is the season for breeding and egg laying. It rained earlier, and when night came,

A Marbled Salamander (photo by the author)

she began moving toward the edges of a small pond where the water level was low. Like salamanders generally, she will find a male and he will deposit a spermatophore on the ground, a little cone containing sperm. During courtship, the female will position herself over the spermatophore and pick up the sperm into her cloaca. Within a few days, she will lay eggs.

Marbled Salamanders have an unusual nesting strategy: they lay eggs in little ponds that have dried up or along the margins of ponds that will later fill with rainwater.[8] Most other species in the mole salamander group lay eggs in the water. When this salamander finds a low place in the ground with only a little water at the bottom, she chooses a spot and pushes the soil around to create a small cavity just below the leaf litter. She begins to lay eggs—first one and then another, until she has produced nearly a hundred eggs. Then, she coils around the nest to brood the eggs. Her movements will turn the eggs over at times, and her body helps keep them from drying out and provides a little protection. It rains a couple of times in the next few weeks, and then after nearly a month, a bigger rainstorm fills the pond up and covers the eggs with water. The water triggers the eggs to hatch. Her job complete, the mother salamander moves on to burrows and places under logs where she can find food.

After hatching, the larval salamanders begin to feed and grow. They feed on tiny animals called zooplankton that float in the water, like copepods and other tiny crustaceans. As they get bigger, these larval Marbled Salamanders look a little like tadpoles, but they have brushy external gills at the back of their heads. They become tiny predators that may eat other larval amphibians. When they reach about an inch in total length, which may take months, they transform into adults.

CHAPTER 6

In the Desert

Gila Monsters, Coachwhips, and Spadefoot Toads

Deserts are areas where there is very little rainfall, generally less than ten inches per year. The United States has three large deserts with hot summertime temperatures: the Chihuahuan, Sonoran, and Mojave Deserts. Imagine yourself walking through the Sonoran Desert of Arizona, over a rocky hillside with big saguaro cacti around you. These are the tall cacti that sometimes look like stick figures with side branches like arms, towering over the desert shrubs.

A "Monster" in Pink and Black

In the Sonoran Desert there is a monster who lives underground much of the time and has a beaded skin of pink or salmon on black. She is pretty easygoing for a monster, but a bite from her would be a very painful medical emergency. She is a Gila Monster, the largest lizard in the United States and the only one with a venomous bite. (A slightly bigger close relative, the Beaded Lizard, lives south of the United States.)

Within a rock crevice, down a little more than two feet where the soil stays cool and slightly damp, the lizard begins to move and flicks her broad tongue, forked a little like that of a snake. It is time to hunt. She climbs to the opening of this burrow, partly shaded by a scrubby mesquite tree. As she comes out into the open, her colors and pattern are bright and pretty. She has a blunt nose and kind of chunky jaws, all covered with black scales. Starting on the top of her head, a pattern of irregular salmon-pink patches mimics the way light would look on the ground when filtered through the thin leaves and branches of mesquite or paloverde. Her scales are rounded and each one contains a little deposit of bone called an osteoderm, giving her a kind of suit of armor. Her tail is thick with fat deposits that can help her go long periods without eating, if she has to. But today she will hunt for nests of eggs or small animals to eat.

She will not wander too far from her burrow under the rock crevice, maybe six or seven hundred feet this evening. For the most part, Gila Monsters are not big travelers. They often live within a home range of about forty acres. Over an entire spring

A Gila Monster (photo by the author)

and summer, a Gila Monster might travel anywhere from less than a mile to more than two miles.[1] Males may move longer distances to look for mates. Today, this one prowls around searching for such things as bird nests, or baby rabbits or rodents. She flicks her tongue, picking up particles to be sensed by the vomeronasal organ, just as snakes do. Slowly working her way around rocks and shrubs, she picks up the scent of a nest of Gambel's quail under a small mesquite. She works her way under the mesquite and takes the first egg into her mouth. The second egg breaks within her jaws, and she laps up the contents. She eats the four additional eggs and then moves on.

In the low light of sunset, moving along an arroyo and back toward her refuge, she is discovered by a coyote. Coyotes do not typically eat Gila Monsters, but this one is curious about the big lizard that smells a little like quail (which he would be happy to eat). She freezes in her tracks as he circles her, trying to figure out what he has found. When he moves in for a closer sniff of her tail, she whirls around with a hiss to face the coyote. She holds her mouth open, exposing the dark gray lining within. She holds her ground, as she is much too slow to make a getaway. When she is faced with an intruder like this, her defense is to hiss and gape her mouth. In the unlikely event that the coyote tried to grab her, she would bite and probably hold on with a viselike grip.

The Gila Monster's sudden threat accomplishes just what it is supposed to—the coyote jumps back a little as the lizard whirls to face him, and after a moment's thought the coyote trots off to search for food somewhere else. After a moment, the lizard turns back toward her burrow within the rock crevice and crawls slowly to it. She found nothing more to eat on her brief walk out in the desert, but the quail eggs will be enough for a while. Gila Monster metabolism (the rate at which they burn energy to keep themselves going) is quite low, so they spend much of their time resting within burrows and crevices. Field research shows that even in active times of year, these lizards spend only about 5 percent of their time aboveground.[2]

THE MONSTER'S BITE

The Gila Monster and beaded lizards are venomous, but there are big differences between these lizards and venomous snakes when it comes to delivering the venom and what it is used for.

Gila Monsters have large, sharp teeth. The ones in the front of the bottom jaw are grooved to allow venom to flow along the teeth and into whatever the lizard is biting. The venom glands are found along the front of the lower jaw, and the venom travels through ducts to be released at the base of the teeth. The venom acts on nerve cells (it is neurotoxic) and produces intense pain. Bites to humans are rare unless the person is handling the lizard, but when a bite does happen, the symptoms include intense pain, very free bleeding, swelling around the bite, weakness or dizziness, anxiety, shortness of breath, fast heart rate, low blood pressure, and other problems. Only a few deaths have occurred, but a person who is bitten needs treatment at a hospital.

Herpetologists have wondered about the primary purpose of the venom. Remember that in snakes, venom is first about getting food, and also about defense. Since Gila Monsters eat primarily eggs and the defenseless nestlings of other animals, it does not appear that they need the venom for catching prey. However, these lizards are big and slow moving, and since their venom produces severe pain, it is thought that they have venom as a defense, not as a way of catching food.

Red Lightning

In a nearby part of the Sonoran Desert, the next morning, a dark serpentine head pokes out of a burrow in the ground. The head and first couple of inches of the neck are black, with irregular flecks or narrow patches of white or red. The sun's warmth is soaked in by the dark color of the snake's head and neck, and he pushes a few inches farther out into the cool desert morning. The black of his neck gradually becomes a pattern of irregular bands of black against a brick-red background. His thermoregulating by sitting in the sun's warmth prepares him for some morning hunting for food. It is as if the sun has charged the engines of speed he relies on for running down the lizards that are a major part of his diet.

He is long and slender, nearly six feet long but not much bigger around than a garden hose. The pinkish red of his midbody continues all the way to his tail, but a curious thing about his pattern makes his tail look like a braided whip. As you look toward his tail, the outer edges of each scale are darker, shading to a pale

A Red Racer, also called a Coachwhip (photo by Troy Hibbitts)

color where the previous scale overlaps it, making the tail look as if it is made of braided strips of red-tinted leather. This species is often called the "coachwhip" because of the appearance of the tail (and this one is also called a "Red Racer").

His eyes are big, as you might expect for a snake that is active during the day and hunts using his vision. The scale above his eye (the supraocular) forms a little bit of a ridge that, from a human point of view, seems to give him a stern, don't-mess-with-me look. However, snakes don't have eyebrows and cannot move their faces around like we can to show a particular mood. Who knows what his mood is today, but he is focused on watching for any lizard that might be moving, or even a big grasshopper that he could chase down and eat. He will also explore crevices and burrows, and if he were to find a mouse, he would eat that as well.

Slipping around rocks, between tufts of grass and through the jumbled sticks of an old packrat den, he moves in graceful curves. The Red Racer pauses and raises his head about a foot off the ground to look around. Like a falcon scanning each detail on the ground below, he focuses on the rocks and the hedgehog cactus below the nearby creosote bush, and then he notices movement just beyond. A Tiger Whiptail lizard is also out looking for food, turning this way and that and checking for insects. It moves by darting ahead a little bit at a time, as if barely restraining an impulse to sprint away. The snake launches himself into action, like red lightning shooting across the ground. The whiptail sprints away, dodging rocks and cacti and pausing to look for movement. Once the lizard stops, the snake slows as well, looking around, scooting forward here and there, and remaining very alert to any movement that would show the location of his prey. At the Red Racer's approach, the lizard instantly darts forward several feet, and that movement brings the snake back into full-speed pursuit. The whiptail darts into a crevice under a rock, and the racer immediately follows. The lizard's shelter is not narrow enough to keep the snake out, and the chase ends with the racer grabbing it in strong jaws. The muscles and jaws of the snake work their way to the lizard's head and begin the process of swallowing. While some snakes use constriction or venom to kill or paralyze what they eat, other snakes must simply grab, hang on, and swallow. Coachwhips and racers such as this one may throw a loop of their body over the prey animal to hold it down, and that may help. However, their jaws are not designed to crush or tear food apart. Instead, they are designed to hang on and stretch forward to pull the prey animal farther into their mouth for swallowing.

A week or so later, the Red Racer's brilliant red and black colors begin to look dull. He stays within his refuge under a big rock. As the days go by, it is as if he has been dipped in a milky substance; the pattern can still be seen, but through a bluish milky haze. The cells within his skin have started the process by which a new outer layer of skin is formed and the old one shed. Because snakes' eyes are covered with a clear scale (the spectacle), his eyes look like milky goggles, making it harder for him to see. That is another reason for him to stay under the rock. Without his vision, he would be nearly defenseless out in the open. He would not see a hawk until the last moment, when the big bird blocked the sun and the talons grabbed his body. The predator of lizards would be the hawk's prey. So instead, he stays in his shelter, and in another day or so his scales are no longer clouded. His body looks nearly normal, except for a slightly dull appearance.

He comes out into the sunlight, cruising among the rocks and pushing his snout against different objects. After a short time, the edge of his outer layer of skin comes loose along his upper lip and the edge of his snout. It begins to peel back from the tip of his lower jaw, too. The snake rubs his snout and jaws along the edge of the rock, peeling the skin back farther. This outer skin turns inside out as the snake pushes forward, and it is damp where it was in contact with the new skin. Once it is peeled back to the eyes, the cap of old skin separates from the new, crystal clear spectacle. The Red Racer begins slowly crawling out of his old skin. At the point where the skin is peeling, his muscles stretch his body to help the layers of skin separate. When he is finished there is a thin, translucent, inside-out copy of the snake, with faint traces of his pattern showing, if you look closely. On the snake himself, the new skin is glossy and the colors and pattern are bright. In sunlight, his scales show a little rainbow iridescence. As time goes by, the scales will begin to show a little wear and tear, and if the racer is eating often he will grow some, and within a few months it will be time to start the shedding process again.

Coachwhips and racers are found all across the southern United States, from California to North Carolina. Those in the western half of the country come in a variety of subspecies, each with a little different color, from the rust and tan of the Western Coachwhip to the reds and blacks of the Red Racer whose story appears above, and there are a few others. The Eastern Coachwhip's body is usually a velvety black for the first third or more, shading into tan, but some individuals are all black.

Listening for the Drumming of Rain

It is night in the Sonoran Desert, at the beginning of July. It has been hot and dry. Plants like cacti that store water look shrunken, showing that their stored water has been mostly used up. The clouds on the horizon have moved across the desert, with distant lightning flashes revealing towering thunderheads. As they get closer, the rumble of thunder grows louder. Lightning flashes nearby, momentarily lighting up the rocky desert. The crack of thunder feels like it shakes the ground.

Buried in the ground, something moves. It has been still for months, waiting without food or water. The vibration from the thunder shakes that stillness a little. On the surface, the clouds begin to dump the moisture they carried in. Big drops of rain hit the ground, and then the downpour starts. The drops hit the ground in a continuous drumming that vibrates down through the soil. Across the desert floor, hundreds of living things claw through the soil toward the surface like a horde of zombies.

However, there is no zombie apocalypse in the Sonoran Desert, at least not on this night! These are Couch's Spadefoot Toads, digging back to the surface to meet the rainfall. They will drink, feed, and quickly find the places where rainfall gathers in pools so they can breed. This is one of the hardest places in North America for an amphibian to survive, and their lives are dominated by what they have to do to keep from drying out or overheating.

Breaking free of her burrow in the soil, one spadefoot hops a few feet and then sits in a puddle. She is drinking after a long time with no water. Instead of drinking in the usual way, frogs and toads drink through their skin, in an area of the thighs and part of the belly that touches the ground when the animal is sitting.[3] The skin there is thinner and richly supplied with tiny blood vessels. As water crosses the skin, it is absorbed into the bloodstream of the frog or toad. After a short time sitting in the puddle, the spadefoot moves on toward a low place where a fairly large pool of water was formed by the rain. These toads have only a short time to breed. During the desert monsoon season, several rainstorms may produce temporary pools, but each one soon begins to dry up in the summer heat. They must lay eggs, and then the eggs have to hatch into tadpoles that grow quickly and are ready to transform into little toads before the pool dries up.

She hops on short, powerful legs. Females of her particular species, the Couch's Spadefoot, have three-inch bodies that are greenish yellow, with a network of black markings over the top of the back and snout. Her big eyes have elliptical pupils like a cat's, closing to an up-and-down slit in bright light. The pupils rarely have to close that tightly because these toads are nocturnal—they come out only at night, when the pupils open to gather as much light as possible. On the bottom of each back foot is a hard, dark ridge in the shape of a sickle. This is the "spade" that gives this group of animals their name. The spade is like the edge of a shovel, and it helps the spadefoot dig down into the soil, as the toad scoops with its back legs and works backward down into the soil.

In her travel toward the low area where male toads are already calling, she pauses to snap up any insect she comes across. That is another thing she must do quickly, while she can be aboveground—eat large numbers of invertebrates, enough to last the eight to ten months she will spend belowground. Once the

A Couch's Spadefoot Toad (photo by the author)

rains end, she and her kind will burrow down two feet or more into the soil. Each one will shed several layers of skin to form a cocoon, helping to hold in moisture during the months of waiting.[4]

But how do they know when to come back up? Conditions change quickly in the desert, and the spadefoots must be able to respond fast. Down there in the soil, how do they know when the rains have come? It takes a while for soil moisture to work its way down to the toads. Researchers have found that it is the vibration from the rainfall, the drumming of big drops of rain, that signals the spadefoots to come to the surface. In a 1980 study, Mark Dimmitt and Rodolfo Ruibal kept spadefoots in three kinds of outdoor enclosures. Some of them were open to the rain, some of them had roofs (so the rain vibration would reach the ground, but not the water), and others were in sealed enclosures (to keep out moisture, scents, and temperature and humidity changes). It turns out that vibration from the rain was enough by itself to bring the toads to the surface.[5]

A coyote is on the hunt after drinking his fill from one of the pools of rainwater. He comes across the Couch's Spadefoot on her way to the breeding pool. The coyote's attention is attracted to the movement of the toad, and he trots over and picks her up in his mouth. He drops her a second later and looks as though he has licked something very bitter and unpleasant, which he tries to get out of his mouth by working his tongue and drooling. One amphibian defense is to produce an irritating substance from glands in the skin, and in some species of amphibians (such as the Cane Toad or the Rough-skinned Newt), it can be quite toxic. In toads generally, these glands are concentrated in warts over much of the back and limbs, and in the lumpy, rounded parotoid glands along the side of the head in some toads. Some frogs have dorsolateral ridges containing lots of the glands that produce toxins. In most species of amphibians, these substances are not dangerous to people, as long as we don't eat them. A human who handles a spadefoot toad and gets the secretions into his or her mouth, eyes, or nose will have a burning sensation and a fit of sneezing. If you handle a frog or toad, make sure your hands are clean beforehand (to protect the frog) and wash your hands afterward (to protect you).

After being dropped by the coyote, the spadefoot continues on to the breeding pool. Males are already scattered around the edge of the pool, inflating their throat pouches with a call that sounds like "wa-a-a-a." It's a little like an unhappy sheep, and not at all romantic from a human perspective. Each male calls, pauses for a couple of seconds as if working up the energy to do it again, and then produces that short, nasal call. He throws his entire being into it—"wa-a-a-a"—as if to say, "Pick me! I am healthy and strong, and my genes would make strong little toads." Female toads approach their chosen males, and egg laying begins. The eggs hatch in about one day, and the tadpoles feed and grow in a race to become little toads before the pool dries. Couch's Spadefoot larvae may metamorphose in as little as eight days, or sometimes more if they have a good food supply and the water holds out.[6] All the adults and juveniles will have to find shelter from the desert heat and be ready to disappear beneath the surface until next year.

CHAPTER 7

On the Plains

Western Diamond-backed Rattlesnakes, Horned Lizards, and Ornate Box Turtles

Much of the central United States is known as the "Great Plains," and before it was mostly plowed and planted with crops, it was dominated by grasslands. Imagine that you are in one of the places where native grasses still grow, near a small rocky hillside. We will take a look at three herp species that can be found on the southern Great Plains.

A Snake with Pits and Rattles

It was cold in the cavity below the rocks and earth, five feet or so below the opening between two big rocks on the hillside. It was cold, but not nearly as cold as it had been outside during the winter snowstorms. Twenty-six snakes passed the winter quietly in that underground cavity: five racers, a coachwhip, three Plains Gartersnakes, and seventeen Western Diamond-backed Rattlesnakes. And now, with a few sunny and mild spring days, the hillside was getting a little bit warmer. The snakes were moving around a little more than they had been, and several rattlesnakes

Matador Wildlife Management Area, on the Rolling Plains of West Texas
(photo by the author)

made their way up through the crevices and spaces between the
rocks, to the surface where the sun shone warmly. Each one coiled
within a few yards of the opening in the hillside, absorbing the
heat of the sun. In the evening, they all retreated into their shelter,
but the next sunny day they were out again. As the days got a little
longer and warmer, the snakes moved farther. The gartersnakes
left early to hunt frogs by a nearby creek. The others spent more
and more time away from the den, and soon the rattlesnakes had
all moved to the areas where they hunted in spring and summer.

One of those rattlesnakes, a male about forty inches long,
had established a home range around a stretch of creek about
three-quarters of a mile away from the den. It wasn't that
the rattlesnake wanted to live at the creek, but there was an
old collapsed barn very near it, and many Cotton Rats built

nests underneath the flat pieces of wood on the ground. Small mammals like rats and mice are the primary diet of the Western Diamondback, with smaller and younger snakes eating primarily mice and the bigger ones eating rats, gophers, and squirrels. This rattlesnake sometimes poked around into Cotton Rat burrows to try to find someone at home, but he also sometimes hunted by ambush. This meant that he would find a path used by the rats by tongue-flicking until he detected one, and then he would sit beside the trail and wait, coiled and ready.

He sat beside a trail at sunset, half hidden behind a clump of grasses. His body was surprisingly well camouflaged. Down his back was the typical pattern of his species, diamond-shaped blotches with dark edges, thinly bordered in a light cream color. Toward the tail, the blotches became narrow and less diamond shaped. At the tail, the brown pattern abruptly changed to black-and-white rings, crowned at the very end by a string of rattles.

A Western Diamond-backed Rattlesnake (photo by the author)

Half covered in last year's tall, dormant grass stems, the snake's pattern seemed at first glance like a dappled pattern of light and shadow. The rattlesnake rested his chunky head on top of his coils, looking toward the rat runway. Even on the head, the pattern helped disguise the snake. A dark diagonal band ran from the top of the face backward through the eye to the corner of the mouth. This mask was edged in the same cream color that bordered the diamonds, breaking up the outlines of the face and head. He faced the trail, watching with elliptical or "cat-eyed" pupils. In addition to his eyesight, he was also able to detect changes in temperature.

Between his eye and nostril, but a little lower on each side of his face, was a small depression or pit. Inside the pit, a thin membrane full of delicate nerve endings was stretched across the opening. The nerve endings were very sensitive to infrared, which is a wavelength of light outside the range we can see. Infrared is emitted by warm objects, so the ability to detect infrared gives a snake the ability to "see" heat. The sensations from the pit organ are transmitted along a cranial nerve to the snake's brain, in the same region that interprets vision.[1] It is thought that these sensations work together so that the heat signature of a rat, for example, is part of what the snake sees. Not only that, but the two pit organs face somewhat forward and their fields of sensitivity overlap, to give "stereoscopic" information about a warm object (stereoscopic vision is what allows us to have depth perception, a three-dimensional perception of what is around us). Among the venomous snakes known as vipers, only a subgroup known as pit vipers have a heat-sensing facial pit. Some boas and pythons have a related kind of heat-sensing pit in some of their lip scales.

As the snake waited, the sun set and it got darker and darker. On this moonless night, the snake had to rely on his pit organs to detect anything that came along the trail. After a bit, a Cotton Rat came along. The rattlesnake remained quite still and when the rat got close enough, the snake struck, injected venom, and pulled back to its coiled position in an instant. The rat jumped and tried to run down the trail but traveled only a short way before falling

HOW THE SNAKE SWALLOWS ITS FOOD

People have always been fascinated with the snake's swallowing ability. Most snakes eat prey much bigger than their heads, and they have to do it with no hands or arms. Snake jaws do not become "unhinged" or "dislocated" during swallowing. Instead, a particular arrangement of skull and jaw bones allows the jaws to open very wide and to move very flexibly.

The snake's quadrate bone, which is a part of the back of the skull in some animals, extends down and back and connects the lower jaw to the skull. Its attachment at the skull can rotate, as can its attachment at the lower jaw. This gives it two hinges, making it possible for the jaws to open very wide.

The three bones of the snake's upper jaw are only loosely connected to the skull and can slide forward and backward independently of the skull. Imagine being able to stretch your upper jaw and teeth forward to take a bite of something in front of your face!

Where the two lower jaws come together in the front, they are joined by soft tissue that can stretch, meaning that the mouth can open very wide.

The recurved teeth (pointed backward) can easily slide forward over a mouse or frog or other prey, but when the jaw is pulled back, the teeth hook into the prey to pull it toward the throat.

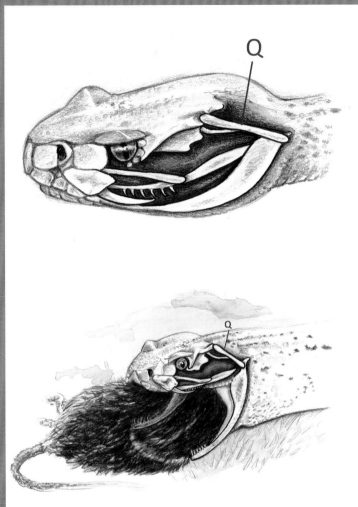

At top, a rattlesnake with mouth closed, cut away to show
the position of the skull, quadrate bone (indicated by the
Q), and jaws. Below, a rattlesnake swallowing a Cotton Rat,
showing how the quadrate bone allows the snake's mouth
to open wider, and how far apart the lower jaws can stretch.
(illustration by Jack Jeansonne)

over. The venom did its work quickly, overwhelming the small mammal's body and beginning to break down its tissues.

The snake followed, tongue-flicking and sensing the chemical trail to find where the rat had gone. When the rattlesnake was convinced that its prey had stopped all kicking and twitching, he began to probe the animal with his snout, looking for the right place to begin swallowing. After a few tongue-flicks at the rodent's nose, the snake opened his jaws and took the rat's head. He stretched the right side of his face forward—the upper and lower jaws simultaneously—and clamped shut and pulled back to the normal position. This hooked the rattlesnake's teeth into the rat and pulled it toward his mouth. Then he did the same with the left side of his face; stretched his jaws forward, closed, and pulled that side of the rat's head farther in. In this way, the snake swallowed the rat, the right side of his head alternating with the left side to pull the prey farther and farther into his throat.

Having swallowed his meal, the Western Diamond-backed Rattlesnake made his way to an abandoned rodent burrow he had used before. He curled up at the bottom of the burrow and rested while his stomach began digesting his meal.

Several days later, he came out of the burrow to bask in the morning sun and then headed down near the creek for a drink of water. Along the creek, various trees and some brush grew, enough to provide shelter for a few White-tailed Deer. Without knowing it, one of them was walking toward the rattlesnake, and as it stepped nearly on him, the snake was startled and pulled back into a defensive coil, instantly beginning to buzz his rattle. The rattle was a warning, a signal that it was dangerous to be there. It was the deer's turn to be startled, and it jumped back and quickly walked away.

The rattle is a series of hollow segments made of the same sort of material that makes fingernails. Part of each segment extends up inside the next one so that they interlock and cannot easily come apart. When the tail shakes, the segments rattle against each other, creating the sound. The shaking is done by specialized muscles in the tail, and when the snake is warm and

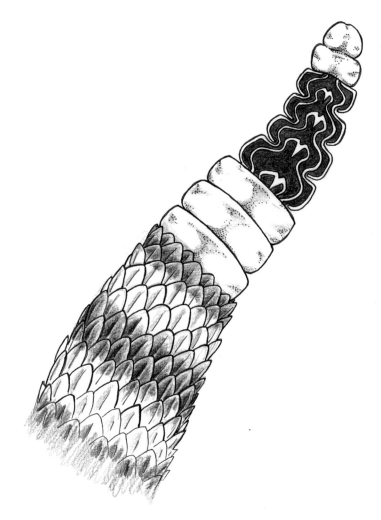

A rattlesnake's rattle, with several segments cut away to show how they interlock (illustration by Jack Jeansonne)

active, the rattle may be vibrated at over sixty cycles per second.[2] The sound has been described as buzzing, or perhaps hissing or sizzling. The tail-shaker muscles are supplied with lots of blood vessels so there is a rich supply of oxygen, allowing the muscles to keep working for a long time without fatigue. Rattlesnakes rattle when they are frightened or threatened, and the rattling stops when the threat goes away and the snake calms.

Baby rattlesnakes are born with a "prebutton"; they soon shed their skin and at that point they have a "button" at the end of the tail. After that, each time the snake sheds its skin, it adds another segment to the rattle. As you can imagine, an older snake might develop a very long rattle string, except that the last segments sometimes get caught between rocks or within brush as the snake travels, and they break off.

The Western Diamond-backed Rattlesnake has a counterpart in the eastern United States, the Eastern Diamond-backed Rattlesnake. They are different species but share a fairly similar pattern, with the eastern species being more brightly marked and having a slightly bigger record size (ninety-nine inches,[3] which is much longer than the average length of either one). There are many other rattlesnakes in the genus *Crotalus*; all of them are pit vipers but they live in many different habitats and have a variety of appearances and life histories.

The Life of the "Horny Toad"

The native grasses on the plains tend to grow in bunches, so that instead of a carpet of grass there are clumps of grasses, sometimes growing close together but always leaving at least a little open ground between them. Here and there you notice a little clearing, an open spot, and sometimes there is a small hole in the middle of it, surrounded by a tiny field of pebbles. Big red ants busily go in and out of that central opening, either bringing bits of leaves or seeds down into the ant colony, or leaving to go gather more. These nearly half-inch-long dark red insects are harvester ants, one of the twenty-two species in the United States that hunt for seeds and other material. If you look, you can find little trails reaching out from the colony in several directions, with worker ants busy finding more food and bringing it home.

Beside one of those trails, a spiky lizard sits. As the ants go by, he moves forward just a bit and laps up some of the insects. From the ant's point of view, the lizard is as imposing as any dinosaur we might imagine. His face is blunt and scaly, with a slight frill at the back of his head, crowned with horns. Two of the horns, at the very center of this frill, are longer than the rest and look quite sharp. Above each small black eye, his skull comes to a point with another short horn. And along his lower jaw is a row of hard, wedge-shaped scales ending in another small spike at the back of his jaw. From ground level, he looks like some armored and fearsome dragon.

The lizard's body is broad and flat, with a fringe of little spines in two rows along the edge. His back is covered with tiny scales and dotted with spines like sharp little pyramids. Some people think that the blunt head, squat body, and short tail give him a toad-like look, so his kind are called "horny toads." The more accurate name is horned lizard, and this one is a Texas Horned Lizard. He is just under four inches long and colored in shades of straw, light reddish brown, and gray to match the surrounding soil and pebbles.

He continues to pick off harvester ants as they come along the trail. Harvester ants are about two-thirds of the Texas Horned Lizard's diet,[4] so he has to eat a lot of them—hundreds per

A Texas Horned Lizard (photo by the author)

day—in order to get enough nutrition. He will eat other insects occasionally, but he does most of his hunting along the harvester ant trail. He does not try sitting at the main entrance to the colony, because the worker ants would rush out and swarm him, and he might be killed. It is much safer to ambush individual ants along their trails.

In the heat of the day, the Texas Horned Lizard seeks shelter in the shade of a clump of grasses or a cactus pad, or perhaps down a burrow. These lizards are adapted very nicely to a life on the hot, semiarid southern plains, and that means that in summer they are more active in the morning and evening. In the morning they can lick dew from vegetation, and they also are able to move the water from raindrops along tiny channels in their skin and to their mouths, "harvesting" the rain as it falls.[5]

In the late afternoon, when the sun is lower and it is not as hot, the Texas Horned Lizard is active again, moving to a different ant colony nearby. He passes another male horned lizard without any response; these lizards are not territorial except during mating season. A month or so ago, he would have treated this other one with head-bobbing displays or pushups to convince the intruder to move on. He would have wanted no competition as he courted female horned lizards. After mating, the female's large body can hold an average of twenty-five eggs.[6] That's a lot, but she needs to produce large numbers because when they hatch, the babies are very small and all their spiky armor is not well developed. Having almost no defense except hiding and blending in with the soil, many babies are eaten. Only a few get to grow up to be adults.

A Gray Fox prowls among the grasses and scrub, looking for food at the end of the day. The horned lizard is looking for shelter here at twilight, and the fox spots his movement. Coming around a mound of cactus, the fox jumps for the lizard and grabs him. A moment later the fox drops the horned lizard and trots off, pausing to rub his snout against the grass as if trying to get a horrible taste out of his mouth. The horned lizard sits on the ground where he was dropped by the fox, some blood smeared on his face. It is the lizard's blood, but he is not hurt. The little reptile squirted the blood from his own eye, in a very strange self-defense tactic.

What happened is that a little pocket or sinus behind each of the horned lizard's eyes filled with blood. His eyelids swelled as the spaces filled up, and then he squirted the blood out of the corner of his eye. The Texas Horned Lizard can shoot this blood up to four feet, either forward or backward.[7] It is very distasteful to members of the dog family like coyotes and foxes, so it is a helpful defense against those animals.[8] It may not be effective against other predators, including some lizards and snakes (which are occasionally found dead with those big horns sticking through their throat), and birds such as the Greater Roadrunner.

This Texas Horned Lizard, living on relatively undisturbed ranchland, is a lucky member of the horned lizard clan. Many older folks (including me) remember a time when these reptiles were common in backyards, parks, and athletic fields in many more places than they are currently found. Over the past forty or fifty years, the range of the Texas Horned Lizard has shrunk, especially from the eastern part of its range. Plenty of old-timers have wondered, "Where did the horny toads go?" (And this is the title of a film you might want to see, if you would like more information about horned lizards and what happened to them.[9]) Many things have contributed to their decline, including loss of native grasslands and other habitats, use of pesticides, and the Red Imported Fire Ant, which horned lizards do not eat.

Along with the Texas Horned Lizard we have just talked about, eight other species of horned lizards are found throughout the western United States and parts of Mexico. One of them, the Greater Short-horned Lizard, gives birth to live young.

The Box Turtle's Home

The next morning, under a fallen tree branch near the creek, a head peeked up from out of the ground. It was a turtle head with a somewhat boxy shape, bright yellow-brown eyes, and a hard beak for biting and cutting. Behind her head, the top of the turtle's shell was visible above the ground. It was dark brown, almost black, with a yellow line down the back and a few short yellow lines on each scute, as if someone had used a yellow marker to trace sun rays radiating from a spot on each one. These markings identified her as an Ornate Box Turtle, a species of box turtle found in the central United States and parts of northern Mexico.[10] She had slept in a scooped-out place in the ground called a "form," a shallow shelter box turtles create by digging into the soil and leaf litter until they are mostly covered.

She was hungry. Pulling out of her form and walking a short distance, she spotted a grasshopper as it shifted its position on a grass stem. The box turtle charged toward the grasshopper, surprisingly fast for a turtle. The grasshopper jumped, landing a few feet away on bare ground, and the turtle took off after it, taking a big, crunching bite as she caught the insect. Swallowing the first treat of the morning, she wandered off looking for

An Ornate Box Turtle (photo by Carl Franklin)

"second breakfast," making her way toward some brushy vegetation near the creek. The hunt for invertebrates was good here, and seasonally the grapevine produced a wonderful, sweet fruit. In their daily movements, box turtles are known to remember landmarks such as sources of water and shelter, fruit trees, and so on. They live their long lives in fairly small areas with which they become very familiar.

As she reached the border of the creek, her attention was caught by an orb-weaving spider settling into position in a low-lying web, ready to ambush the next insect caught in the web. The box turtle charged toward the spider, but the spider was too nimble, moving to a higher part of the web and out of reach. And so she moved on, alongside some bushes where she nibbled the tender shoots of a plant and munched a mushroom.

As a deer wandered too close, the box turtle retracted into her shell with a quick hiss as she exhaled, making room for all of her body within the shell. The lower shell—the plastron—of box turtles is hinged so that the front and back lobes can be pulled up against the edges of the carapace (upper shell) when the turtle hides protectively. It is a good thing they can get by for a while with minimal breathing, because with everything pulled within the shell, there is not much room to expand the lungs and take a breath. After nothing else happened for a couple of minutes, the front of the plastron began to lower a little, like a tailgate being dropped just enough to peek out. Seeing no threat, she fully opened her shell and began to walk. She knew where she was going in the fifteen or so acres she called home. Like most box turtles, she stayed within a relatively small area called a "home range."

Three species of box turtles are recognized in the United States: the Florida Box Turtle, Eastern Box Turtle, and Ornate Box Turtle. The Three-toed Box Turtle, a subspecies of the Eastern Box Turtle, is considered by some to be a separate species. Names change, but turtles remain the same!

DON'T TRANSPLANT A TURTLE!

People sometimes think they can help a turtle find a better home, or they would like to try to reestablish box turtles where they once lived. Sometimes they have a pet box turtle that they no longer want, and they imagine that if they release it in the woods somewhere, it will be fine. Chances are that it may not be fine. Turtles remember the landmarks where they live, and they will generally try to find those landmarks if we take them somewhere and let them go. Here are a few facts about turtle travels:

Box turtles have a sort of internal "clock," letting them know roughly what time of day it is. This lets them use the position of the sun like a compass. For example, if it is early morning, the sun should be in the east, and they can use the position of the sun to know in what direction to go. They also have some ability to use the earth's geomagnetic field to help move in the right direction.

If moved out of their home range, most often they will use those abilities to try to find familiar landmarks. While some may stay in the area where they are released, many will wander off. Adults are especially likely to stay on the move, while hatchlings or juveniles may be more likely to establish a new home range.

While moving in unknown places, preoccupied with finding home, box turtles may run into hazards such as roads, dogs, or poor habitat, or they may simply not find enough food or shelter.

Because box turtles so often do not settle down in a new place, most people do not think that releasing them (especially adults) away from home is a workable conservation strategy.

CHAPTER 8

Finding and Observing Them

The previous chapters give you a glimpse of herps you might see in the creek, the woods, and lots of other places. If you think finding them in these natural settings might be the ideal way to do it, great! It is good to see them in zoos, and you can learn a lot by watching them in a good nature show on TV. However, seeing them "in person," in the places they live, gives them a reality and an excitement that I don't believe you will find anywhere else.

Almost anywhere you live in the United States, you are probably not far from places you could see reptiles and amphibians. Despite its isolation, Hawaii has a few herps such as sea turtles, the rarely seen Yellow-bellied Sea Snake, and a few other species that have been introduced. A few of the sea turtles may be seen on the coast of Alaska, and it has a handful of frogs and salamanders. The lower forty-eight states have many species (Texas, for example, has 284 kinds of herps[1]). They live in preserves, parks, ranchlands, and forests, and a few might live in your backyard. In many places, fences, sheds, and trees in your yard or the park may have fence lizards or spiny lizards. Don't be too quick to catch them! Watching them grab an insect and run back up to their favorite perch can be entertaining. Find out whether there are gartersnakes or the related Dekay's Brownsnakes or Red-bellied Snakes in local parks or nearby woodlands. Look for toads near the garden at night and listen for frogs calling after rains.

The backyard or local park may be a great place to start, but you may soon find that you are hungry for more kinds of herps and more places to see. As you think about expanding your herping activities, make sure that you also expand your skills. Some skills will help you successfully find herps and know which kind you have found. Other skills will help keep you safe. Let's talk about some of the kinds of experiences and training that I believe are important to give you those skills.

Time in the Field

This is where it gets real. For many people, this is where you begin to love nature and all its plants and animals, including herps. What will be around the next bend or in the next tree? You expect something wonderful and enjoy the uncertainty of what it will be. The more you get to know a place, the more you find little things to appreciate even when you don't find something "big." The field is a great teacher—it is patient and willing to be there with you even if you don't get it at first. It rewards your efforts with discoveries to match what you're looking for— lovely and interesting colors and designs, intellectual insights, adventure and accomplishment.

For these reasons, a person who wants to learn about field herpetology (or the study of birds or any other field of study concerning animals or plants) should start in the field and return to it often. It is good to do this with a couple of people who share your interest. You really should do it with a mentor, someone who already knows what to do in the field. This is someone who is skilled enough to be safe and successful and who can support your curiosity and joy as you learn.

Knowing the Different Species and Their Habits

At the same time as you are getting out in the field, you should learn how to identify some of the reptiles and amphibians that

A good herping spot: the Lyndon B. Johnson National Grasslands in Wise County, Texas (photo by the author)

live where you are exploring. Get a good field guide covering your area. There are many good guides for states or regions, but you might start with the one by Robert Stebbins and Samuel McGinnis[2] covering western North America, or the one by Robert Powell, Roger Conant, and Joseph Collins[3] covering eastern North America. Earlier editions of these books are classics that many of us carried in our backpacks and on our car dashboards for years. It feels good to know what kind of turtle you saw basking in the pond, or which treefrog was clinging to a tree branch, but identification skills are particularly needed when venomous snakes may be present in your area. You should know that not every one of them will look like the photo in the field guide. There are normal variations in pattern and color, and then there is the occasional snake whose pattern is very different because of some genetic mutation. The more experience you have, the better you will be at recognizing a species based on its overall form and shape as well as color and pattern.

Another kind of skill is knowing the habits of different herps, such as when they are most active, what they eat, and the habitats where they are found. There are reptiles that actively hunt prey during the day, relying on their keen vision and ability to chase insects or lizards. There are those that lie in wait, camouflaged in leaf litter and hidden in the dark of night, ready to ambush a passing mouse. Some spend most of their time underground or under rocks and logs, while others live in trees. Our largest salamander, the Hellbender, requires fast-flowing rocky streams, but another large salamander, the Mudpuppy, can live in slow, murky water. If you want to see these animals, it's important to know their lifestyles.

How to Search for Herps

As you walk in the woods or wade in the creek, the herps might come to you, but for the most part you have to search for them. There are several ways to do this.

First, be quiet and focused as you scan the places where reptiles and amphibians might be. I don't mean to say that you can't relax and talk some of the time, but you will be more likely to miss things if you are distracted. As you walk or wade, think about the species that live in that habitat. Will some of them be basking on rocks or tree trunks? Will they be actively looking for food? Or will they be under a shelter such as a log or rock? These questions will get you looking in the right places. Keep in mind that every time you spot a lizard or frog or other herp, you are training your brain how to look for them. People talk about this as developing a "search image" for each animal, so that you can recognize a partly hidden or camouflaged animal because your brain "knows how to see it." That is one of the ways a mentor can be helpful, by pointing out animals you might miss.

At the same time that you are looking at exposed rock ledges, tree trunks, or the edge of a pond or marsh, you should also be looking where you step. This is especially true if you are off the trail. It is easier to see whether there is a snake or frog on the bare ground of a trail, and it is much harder in tall grass or alongside a fallen log. I remember walking in some thin grasses in a spot in West Texas and suddenly hearing a rattlesnake's rattle beginning to twitch and make noise, though it was not yet a full buzz. The snake was clearly within a few steps of me, and I stood very still until my friends and I determined where it was. We found it, and everyone got to walk away (or crawl away, in the case of the snake) with no harm done. However, this example shows how important it is to pay attention to where you are walking.

Herps are often under some sort of cover, like a flat rock, a discarded sheet of plywood, or a log. So, herpers often lift these objects to see what may be underneath. You could get a lot of exercise lifting (or "flipping," in the language of field herpetology)

Discarded plywood can provide an excellent refuge for herps (photo by the author)

every loose object you find, but I hope you won't. Think about the needs and behavior of the animals you are looking for. They may want something that insulates against extreme temperature (bigger is better) or something that warms up quickly in the morning sun (sheets of tin lying on the ground are perfect). They want something with some space underneath, like a flat rock rather than a round boulder embedded in the ground.

Now before you flip that piece of tin or flat rock, stop and think. If you are a scorpion or a copperhead under there and you get poked by a finger, you're going to defend yourself. Don't get hurt! Either grab the object where you can see everything near your fingers or use a hook. This is probably the primary use for what is called a "snake hook." It is shaped kind of like an L and can be slipped under a snake's body to lift it and move it somewhere. However, in the field a snake hook is most often used to lift things that herps may be hiding under. Slip the hook under the object on the side *away from you*. That way, when you lift it, your feet are not exposed to whatever may be underneath.

Here is another thing to think about before you flip a rock

Ki shows the proper use of a snake hook to lift a rock (photo by the author)

or log. Herps use a particular piece of cover because it provides the right temperature and humidity and offers them the right amount of room. Not just any old log will do, and not every rock catches just the right amount of sun or has the right size opening under it. When we flip rocks or logs, we may make them unusable for herps. A decaying log may come apart when we turn it, and we may not put a rock back in exactly the same place it was resting. Some careless people just flip cover over and leave it where it lands. Researchers in Australia carefully observed whether herps used rocks that were left out of place and found that they did not.[4] A rock that had been carefully put back in its original position was much more likely to be used by lizards and snakes. They also found that the temperature and humidity were different under rocks that humans had moved. So, my suggestion is this: if moving something will destroy it, the decision should almost always be to leave it alone; and if you do flip the object, put it back *exactly* as it was. The herps, and future visitors to that site, will thank you.

Catch Them or Just Observe?

So here you are, standing in front of some magnificent reptile or amphibian. What do you do? Its beauty, the delicacy or power of its movement, or something else about it may make you want to hold it or even take it home. Is there any reason you should not? Well, yes, there are several reasons that just watching and not interfering with it could be the best thing. But before laying out those reasons, let me say that I know about the desire to catch them and collect them. Been there, done that. Starting with that first gartersnake when I was ten, I have caught a lot of herps over the years and taken a number of them home. Some of the time, I don't think I did much harm, but here are some ideas I wish I had considered back then:

1. Have you identified the animal, and can it hurt you?
This is hugely important, of course. If it is a pretty
snake and you are almost sure it is a Hog-nosed Snake
but it kind of has reddish bands like a copperhead, leave
it alone! Wait until you have the experience and skills
to be completely sure it is harmless before picking it up.
Similarly, a big Snapping Turtle is a cool animal, and
getting your friend to take a photo of you holding it
sounds great. But unless you know how to capture and
hold it correctly, you may get a very painful bite. If you
pick it up by the tail, you may harm the turtle. Either
one of those things is a bad outcome, so until you have
the training and experience, don't pick it up!

2. Is it legal to pick it up or collect it?
A number of species are protected by law because they
are threatened or endangered. Suppose you are in
southwestern New Mexico and find a brown, vaguely
spotted snake in a creek. If it is a Narrow-headed
Gartersnake it is federally protected, and that means
you cannot capture it or take it home.[5] Or suppose
you visit Shenandoah National Park in Virginia and
find a pretty salamander with a reddish stripe down
its back. It is probably a Shenandoah Salamander, and
it's also federally protected. Not only is there a federal
list of protected species, but each state maintains a list
of species that are in trouble and are protected from
being harmed or collected. States may also regulate
the collection of wildlife, even common species. For
example, in Texas you need a hunting license to pick
up or take home a reptile or amphibian, regardless of
your age. Once you have that license, there are many
species of herps you can collect. You can see which
animals are federally protected by checking with the
US Fish and Wildlife Service. To find out which ones

are protected in your state, check with your state wildlife agency.

3. Is the herp living in a preserve, park, or other protected place?

Don't capture herps if you are in preserves or other such places, even if the animal is common, and even if you have the license or permit that would let you pick it up. These places are refuges where many native plants and animals can live in healthy numbers. Do not assume that they must have plenty of the kind of herp that you found and can easily cope with losing one. Small preserves are easily affected by any kind of disturbance. Other preserves may have lots of visitors just like you who think taking one won't hurt anything, but if everyone thinks like that, lots of animals will be lost. You may think that the animal you want to take home will be comfortable and well fed, so no harm is done. However, here is the way to think about collecting: the animal taken might as well be dead, as far as the remaining population is concerned. There is one less individual of that species in that place, and that's the important thing. In big healthy populations, losing a few will not matter. However, I hope you will help parks, preserves, and refuges stay healthy by remembering that the living things there are not yours for the taking.

4. Have you thought about and made a plan for keeping a herp before collecting it?

Some herps have very specialized diets that you may not be able to provide, or they need plenty of space and exposure to natural sunlight that is difficult to provide. Many a reptile has slowly starved because it was not kept under the conditions it required to eat or was not offered the right food. Others have escaped from cages that seemed OK until a reptilian escape artist was placed in it. On the other hand, many species have diets that are easy to provide, and they can do well for years if you learn what you need to know about how to keep them.

People may also collect specimens to donate to scientific collections at universities or museums. That is a different topic, and the ethics of such collecting are a different discussion. If this is an interest of yours, have that discussion with a professional involved in research or scientific collections.

Lots of decisions, judgments, and skills are needed when you decide to capture a herp, and I'm convinced that the best way to learn how to pick one up and hold it is by watching a mentor and being guided as you try it. Books can get you ready, but a book cannot watch you and give you feedback as you do it. So, if you want to catch snakes, turtles, and other herps, find a good mentor!

You might want someone to teach you how to catch something in the field for a number of reasons. You might capture it in order to get a close look and then immediately let it go. One reason might be to get a precise identification of it. This might happen if you are already sure it is safe to catch, and you need a close observation to tell it apart from a similar species. For example, if you are near the edge of a creek in Texas and spot a slender dark snake about two feet long, with three yellow or yellow-orange stripes, it is very likely that it is either a ribbonsnake or a gartersnake. You might capture it in order to look for black edges on the light-colored lip scales and see whether the lateral stripes (the ones on the sides) are on the second, third, and fourth rows of body scales. That would help you identify it as a Texas Gartersnake.

Another reason to capture it only for a minute or two would be to get a good photograph. If a box turtle is partly dug into the soil and leaf litter, you could get a photo of the back half of the shell. Briefly capturing it might allow you to get a photo of the whole turtle. Sometimes a very active harmless snake like a

HOW I LEARNED TO CATCH HERPS (AND JUST OBSERVE THEM)

In the 1960s, I found a sort of second home at what was then called the Fort Worth Children's Museum. I spent tons of time there with other teenagers eager to learn more. A couple of staff members were the perfect match to show us all about herps. We hung out with the staff in the live animal room, watching and then trying out our own ability to handle frogs, salamanders, and nonvenomous snakes. We went on field trips to several locations where we watched our mentors capture specimens in the field. This is how I learned how to apply what I learned in books and field guides to the "real world." We waded in streams and caught turtles and watersnakes. We flipped sheets of tin over to discover hidden treasures such as a Great Plains Ratsnake on a hillside southwest of Fort Worth. I owe a huge debt to people like John Preston and Rick Pratt for showing me how it was done. They also gave me an appreciation for just watching an animal without capturing it. These experiences enabled some of us to go on to distinguished careers as plant ecologists or conservation scientists. The rest of us were inspired and our lives changed for the better, even if we took different jobs. If that sounds like just what you want, look around for museums, nature centers, or other organizations that offer nature programs. You might find someone who can teach you what you need to know about herps and the rest of the natural world—remember that it's all connected. If you are open to learning (not just showing what you already know) and want to understand herps in depth, you may find someone to teach you who will be generous with his or her time and will treat you as a very important and valued person, because that is exactly what you are!

racer will settle down if placed on the ground under your cupped hands or under a hat. With luck, when you move your hands (or the hat), the snake will sit still briefly for a photograph.

Remember that it is often better to just observe without capturing. Use binoculars for viewing animals that you cannot get very close to or those that would be disturbed if you approached very close. A telephoto lens on your camera can serve the same purpose. Venomous snakes can be observed and photographed from about ten feet away, if you are on solid footing and can move away if you need to. Sometimes a venomous snake sits still at first but then "makes a break for it," heading toward where it thinks it will be safe. It may not matter if you are in its path; it might move toward you as it tries to head for safety. If you step out of the way, it will not try to chase you.

A Five-lined Skink, which is hard to tell apart from a Broad-headed Skink without looking at the lip scales close up. However, it is easy to break off the tail when you try to capture it. (photo by the author)

Can You Let Them Go Later?

Let's say you catch a box turtle somewhere and you keep it for a few months. Some people catch an animal (or someone gives it to them), and after a while what seemed like a treasure now becomes just a chore. Your turtle requires a varied diet and needs exposure to direct sunlight for its vitamin D metabolism, and your initial excitement about it may wear off. Can you let it go? There are several reasons you should not.

1. You may not be able to let it go where it belongs.
Does that species already live where you plan to release it? If you are very far from where it was caught, it may not. Even if you do release it fairly close to where it came from, the habitat may be different. Different soils or availability of water, different things to eat, and different amounts of leaf cover from shrubs or trees are among the things that could doom your released herp to an early death.

2. It is probably outside its home range.
Herps get to know the area where they grow up and tend to stick around within an area called the "home range." Some do very poorly if moved. Box turtles are among the reptiles that often do not settle in to a new place and may wander around without finding suitable shelter or food.

3. It might introduce disease into animal communities where it is released.
You might have taken good care of your box turtle, but often the stress of captivity keeps a herp's immune system from working as well against bacteria, viruses, or fungi. Once they are not held in check, these microorganisms may take over, and then when the animal is released, the disease might be spread through

stools, shed skin, or secretions.[6] Herps in captivity also sometimes pick up infections from other captive animals, and these might be spread. Diseases such as chytrid fungus or ranavirus could be spread from the released herp to other reptiles or amphibians and cause die-offs.

If you have a native reptile or amphibian that you have kept for a while but no longer want to keep, here are a couple of possibilities. If the animal is healthy, you might check around to see whether a nature center would like to have it for educational or display purposes. You also might check with a local herpetological society and see whether one of the members would like to take it.

I mention all these problems that can come from collecting and later releasing herps in order to help you make responsible decisions. Remember I said that I have collected herps myself, and I don't mean to say that no one should ever take a frog or a snake home. However, if you collect it, you assume responsibility for its life. I hope you will decide wisely and do as little harm as possible to the reptiles and amphibians that live in the wild.

CHAPTER 9

Planning Trips and Staying Safe

It's time to get out there and have fun! But I have to include a few pages about planning ahead and staying safe, because it's hard to have fun if you don't take what you need, and it's definitely no fun if you get hurt.

What to Wear and What to Bring

What should you wear and what should you bring when you are out in the field? It's important to wear comfortable and protective clothes. Your exact choices about shoes, pants, and so on might depend on where you are going—particularly whether you will be wading as opposed to hiking. Generally, even on hot days, I suggest jeans or other pants that resist thorns and "bugs." Shorts might be cooler on a hot day, but jeans will keep your legs from being sunburned and you will not get scratched up by briars and thorns. I also think that hiking boots make longer walks more comfortable and give needed ankle support. On the other hand, for wading in a creek, inexpensive and washable sneakers can be good (bring dry socks). Most days, I'm likely to wear a hat with a brim that gives some protection from bright sun and also from light rain.

Backpack, boots, and snake hook (photo by the author)

You should spend some time planning what to take along on your outing. Bring the right amount of stuff—enough to do what you need to do, but not so much that you are weighed down. Here are some important things to consider bringing:

- **Backpack**—Depending on how many things you bring, this may be very important. It should be lightweight and water resistant, with pockets and places for a phone and/or camera, notebook, keys, and a water bottle.
- **Water**—Did I mention that the backpack should hold a water bottle? Water is easy to forget at the beginning of a hike but can be very important. People often recommend that you have one liter of water (that's roughly one quart) for

every one to two hours of hiking, and in some circumstances you might need more.

- *Insect repellent*—This will cut down on problems with mosquitos and ticks, but it's no guarantee against them. Don't handle wildlife with repellent on your hands. Note that the ingredient picaridin, found in some repellents, has been associated with the death of salamander larvae.
- *Phone and/or camera*—A phone will let you contact others if a problem arises or you need to check in. A smartphone lets you use iNaturalist, which I encourage you to do. A camera (either in the phone or a separate one) is great for recording what you see.
- *Map and GPS*—It's important to find your destination and avoid getting lost. If your phone does not have a mapping app, preferably with GPS location, consider downloading one or using a paper map. Get a local trail map if you can.
- *Notebook*—Some people keep their field notes by using iNaturalist, and that's OK. However, a small notebook allows more flexibility for what you want to write or sketch. Something small, like 6 × 9.5 inches, is good. Put it—and a pen or pencil—in a plastic bag.
- *First aid kit*—A small kit with bandages, tweezers, antiseptic wipes, and so on is good to have with you. Include any medicines that you are likely to need while out in the field.
- *Binoculars*—These can help you identify turtles basking away from shore, a wary lizard that keeps its distance, birds, and other wildlife.
- *Digital thermometer*—This allows you to document the temperature at the places you visit.
- *Dip net*—For trips to creeks and marshes, this

can let you sample what's living in the water. A small, easy-to-carry one is best. Clean the net with a bleach solution between trips so you do not transfer microorganisms and algae from one location to another.

- **Walking stick or snake hook**—These can help with balance on uneven ground and can be used to lift something to see what is underneath.

Capturing and Sharing the Experience

I hope you can be absorbed in the experience of what you see and feel and hear, without thinking too much about texting or posting on social media. Your time in the field will be deeper and stick with you longer if you spend most of that time living in the moment. On the other hand, it is good to have some notes and

Taking a camera along allows you to bring back images of beautiful herps like this American Bullfrog (photo by the author)

photos to help you remember the experience, so you could stop periodically to preserve it.

Even with all the technology to help us, there is something to be said for keeping a paper notebook. Some people use a field notebook to jot down only a few things: date, time, state and county, and locality. When they see something they write: "4/7/14, Randall Co., TX. Palo Duro Canyon. 11:30am, adult male side-blotched lizard. Air temperature 87°F." Other people treat the field notebook more like a diary or journal. After noting the date, county, location, and time, they might write: "Along the canyon wall, where a shelf of rock dropped off, an adult male side-blotched lizard was basking on a rock slab. He looked over his shoulder at us, but we had time to admire the little blue speckles over his back and down his tail, and we took a photo before he darted off. The air temperature was 87°F." I don't think there is a right way and a wrong way, although more diary-style

Adult male Side-blotched Lizard, April 7, 2014, Palo Duro Canyon, Randall County, Texas (photo by the author)

A LOOK AT BOX TURTLES IN NORTH TEXAS USING INATURALIST

To give you an idea about how the observations contributed by citizen-scientists might be used, I looked at observations of the Ornate Box Turtle on the iNaturalist website. I chose eleven counties surrounding Dallas and Fort Worth to see what I could learn about how often, where, and when they are seen. On the iNaturalist website, I clicked "Explore" and then entered "Ornate Box Turtle" in the "Species" search field, and then the county name in the "Location" field. Here is what I learned:

> Ornate Box Turtles were reported a total of forty-three times. The first observation was in August 2011 and the most recent was in May 2019, just before I looked at the records. Over half of the observations were in 2017 and 2018 (and there were no sightings in 2012 or 2013). We cannot use that to say that box turtles are becoming more numerous. Unlike a scientific experiment where we make sure that our observation methods are the same from one year to the next, in this case it could be that more people were looking in more places in the last couple of years, as iNaturalist has become more popular. More "effort"—that is, a greater number of people reporting—should explain the increased numbers, as iNaturalist became more popular in Texas after about 2013.
>
> I sorted the observations by month and found that these turtles were reported most often in May and June (fourteen and eleven sightings, respectively). Those are months in which Ornate Box

Turtles are mating and finding places to lay eggs, so it makes sense that they would be seen more often while moving around.

Most sightings (86 percent) were in the western counties of the area I sampled, and that may reflect a couple of things. Ornate Box Turtles tend to be found in more upland areas, including grasslands and savannas, and there is more of that habitat from about Fort Worth westward. Additionally, the places where box turtles might live are more developed and crisscrossed by roads in the urban and eastern counties, and there is still a little more ranchland and less-developed habitat to the west.

Suppose someone looks at all the observations of these turtles or studies the sightings throughout an entire ecoregion of the state. Chances are, they can learn a lot about how often Ornate Box Turtles are being seen, or where they are still common. And if you contribute some observations, you could help make it happen!

An Ornate Box Turtle seen on a road in the LBJ National Grasslands near Fort Worth, Texas, in May of 2018 (photo by the author)

notes may help you recall the moments in more detail years later when you want to relive that trip.

Technology does have its virtues, and among them is the iNaturalist app, which connects you with fellow naturalists, experts who can help you identify what you see, and a database of plants and animals with locations where people have found them.[1] Here's how it works: suppose you see that side-blotched lizard but you don't know what it is. Using your phone's camera within the app, you take a photo and log it as an observation. The app uses your phone to show the date, time, and GPS location. You can add information about the temperature, surroundings, or other conditions. If all you know is that it is a lizard, then just identify it as "lizard." The app will attempt to match the photo with its database to suggest what may be the right species. If you post the observation under any of a number of projects, one or more experts will look at your observation and help verify what it really was. At that point, your observation becomes part of a database of observations that researchers can use to help answer questions like these: At what time of day are Common Side-blotched Lizards most often seen in Palo Duro Canyon? From one year to the next, are they being found more often, less often, or with about the same frequency? Not only will you help out as a citizen-scientist, but your observations will be saved under your profile so you can look them over later to remember what you saw. What if you are using a separate camera (maybe with a zoom to see that lizard up close)? If you enter an observation without a photo in the field, you can go back and upload a photo later on a desktop computer. Just log in to your iNaturalist account and add whatever you like to your observation.

Preparing for Trips or Even Short Walks

Here are some things to do when planning any outing, to be prepared and to keep a small problem from becoming a big problem. These precautions apply to short trips as well as longer ones, because accidents can happen even at a local park. The very idea of herping is that you are going to places where you are more isolated, because that's where most herps are. Even on a short walk, you are more than just a few steps away from the car and there are probably no helpful bystanders nearby.

- Tell someone specifically where you are going and when you will check back with them.
- For longer trips, go with at least one other person. I know people who have taken a last-minute trip to Big Bend with the idea of driving back roads at night to look for snakes. It worked out OK for them, but it might not have. Visiting a remote area such as this always involves some risk, and you shouldn't do it alone.
- Take the backpack described earlier. If you are walking for just a few minutes, a short distance from your car, at least take your phone and have the backpack in your car. Remember that for field herping the backpack is important not because you need food and shelter for a long backcountry trip, but rather so you will be prepared to get information (like temperature) and record your observations, and to take care of things like getting a minor cut or being thirsty.
- Check the weather at your destination and along the way. Is there a likelihood of anything like flash floods or strong storms? Will the weather be good for herping? Reschedule, if you need to.
- If going to a preserve, check to make sure it will be open. I once traveled to the Lower Rio Grande Valley with a friend, and one of the main goals was to visit the Sabal Palms Sanctuary there. When we arrived at the gate, we found out the sanctuary was closed for maintenance that

month. Luckily there were several other nearby destinations we wanted to visit.

Venomous Snakebite

Those who love reptiles may take a "no fear" approach to venomous snakes, and perhaps that is OK as long as it doesn't mean "no care" and "no respect." Most of the states of the United States have one or more species of dangerously venomous snakes, and while these snakes don't want to hurt you, if they feel threatened they *can* hurt you, and some could kill you. As long as you are careful and respect them enough not to take chances or do something stupid, there is no real need for fear. Being careful means following the guidance provided in the previous chapter and always looking where you step and put your hands. Respecting the snake means not "pushing the limits"—not taking

Avoid accidentally putting your hands or feet near venomous snakes like this Broad-banded Copperhead (photo by the author)

foolish chances and not letting yourself get too confident or too sure that everything will go according to plan.

For a person in the United States, being bitten in the field by a venomous snake is uncommon. Take alcohol and daredevil stunts out of the equation, and venomous snakebite is even more uncommon. Daniel Keyler reported that in 2009 there were 3,582 cases of venomous snakebite in the United States. Of those, only three were fatal.[2] Chances are, you will not be bitten, and if you are, your chances of surviving the bite are very high.

When humans are bitten by venomous snakes, sometimes little or no venom is injected. This is called a "dry bite." One estimate is that 20 to 25 percent of pit viper bites in the United States involve either no venom or so little that no real symptoms develop.[3] Some sources report fewer dry bites; one group in Arizona estimated that only about 3 percent of bites are dry.[4] If you are bitten by a snake that may be venomous, do not let wishful thinking lead you to say "maybe it's a dry bite"—don't delay getting help.

Ordinarily, a pit viper bite in which venom is injected (an envenomation) will hurt with a sharp, burning pain. An envenomation from a coralsnake may not hurt much, although sometimes people report a lot of pain. Coralsnakes, like their relatives the cobras and kraits, have venom that attacks the nervous system, with much less of the bruising, swelling, and pain that come from pit viper bites. And the venom of a few pit vipers has enough neurotoxins that there may not be much initial pain. You should not decide whether a snakebite is venomous according to the amount of pain you feel!

Let's talk about what you should do in case you are bitten by a snake that you identify as venomous, or that you think could be venomous. We'll start with what *not* to do. In past years there have been all kinds of ideas about first aid for snakebite in the field, and physicians found that most of them didn't help and could even make things worse. Since I am not a physician, I am going to report recommendations by experts; none of the opinions are my own. First, do not take any medicine unless directed by a physician. For example, do not take aspirin or related medicines like ibuprofen that can complicate bleeding problems.[5] Practice guidelines from the Wilderness Medical Society[6] give further guidance about what not to do for pit viper bites, including the following: do not use a tourniquet or anything to restrict blood supply; do not cut into the bite and try to suck venom out; and do not use a mechanical extractor to try to remove venom.[7] Do not apply ice to the bite, and do not apply electricity (shock) to it. Researchers and physicians have found that these things do not work, even though we might wish they did.

Here is what you *should* do if you are bitten by a snake that you think is venomous, again drawing on the Wilderness Medical Society's practice guidelines and other authorities. Move away from the snake, and if you can quickly take a photo to help confirm its identity, do so. However, do not waste valuable time trying to hunt the snake down to photograph it (or kill it). Do not try to take the snake along—either alive or dead—for positive identification; the person bitten will be able to get proper treatment because it will be based on his or her symptoms.

Immediately take rings and other jewelry off the patient, because one of the primary symptoms of pit viper bites is severe swelling. Rings or bracelets will do a lot of harm because they restrict blood flow, worsening the pressure and depriving tissues of oxygen, so get them off right away. Do not let the bitten person exert themselves, as this pumps the venom through the body more quickly. Calm them and reassure them that they will get through this.

At this point the main thing you need to do is get the person to the hospital. That part is crucial, since the treatment of venomous snakebite is mostly about using *antivenom* to neutralize the snake venom and to treat the complications of snakebite, including problems with blood pressure, clotting time, and other problems.[8] Except in the worst circumstances, the patient should not be allowed to drive, because even though at first there may just be pain and swelling around the bite, the person's condition can worsen rapidly.

It is helpful to use a pen to mark the edge of the swelling on the skin and write the time there as well. The goal is for a treating physician to know how the swelling has progressed over time. At first, the swelling might involve just a finger, and later the whole hand, and still later some of the forearm, and so on. A helpful smartphone app is SnakeBite 911,[9] which you can use to dial 911, call Poison Control (they can provide expert advice to patients and physicians about symptoms and treatment), take photos of the bite location and swelling, and locate the closest hospital. Hang on to the toll-free Poison Control number if you are not using the SnakeBite 911 app—the number is 800-222-1222.

Remember, chances are if you get the knowledge and experience you need and use good judgment, you are probably not going to be bitten. And if despite your knowledge and experience you do get bitten, chances are you will recover. Don't let fear of venomous snakes frighten you away from spending time in the field—just be prepared, as you would be for any other emergency.

CHAPTER 10

Your Mission, If You Choose to Accept It

At this point, after reading the previous chapters, you know a lot about reptiles and amphibians, and you may be planning some outings to look for them. I hope you have the most wonderful time possible while you are out there! Walking through a woodland or wading in a creek and seeing these animals is a real privilege. The beauty of the colors and patterns is amazing if you stop for a minute, clear your mind, and take it all in. So are the sounds—frog calls, birdsongs, the sighing of the breeze, and the humming of insects. And of course, the intellectual puzzles, wondering "how did it get this way?" or "how does this animal do that?" You think about these things and then you can read and learn from those who came before you, and maybe your observations will add to our knowledge of natural history. All in all, you may have wonderful experiences ahead of you. But there's something else, a challenge for you if you choose to accept it.

As you know, reptiles have been around for over 200 million years, and amphibians for even longer. Their "family tree" has produced an amazing variety of animals, with amazing abilities and defenses. However, we are living in a time when reptiles and amphibians are found in smaller numbers and in fewer places.[1] Some species are gone and we will never see them again.

The world changes and all plants and animals go through hard times and good times. In the continuous unfolding of life on earth, some species die off as others are born. Is this what is happening to herps? Is this just the normal process of life, or is it something else? Do we have any control over what is happening here?

Species die off when they can no longer "make a living" in the places they live. When they cannot find suitable food or shelter, or the winters are too cold or the summers too hot, they die off. When some disease or predator overwhelms their defenses, they die off. It turns out that a lot of the ways herps are being overwhelmed are a result of what we do. The ways in which we use the land and our economic activities have big impacts on nature. Here are some of the things scientists have listed as the most important threats to herps:[2]

- *Habitat loss.* The places herps live are being destroyed or changed so the animals cannot live there. Wetlands are drained, forests cut down, and grasslands plowed, and the animals that lived there disappear. Roads cut through habitat and huge numbers of reptiles and amphibians are killed as they try to cross.
- *Pollution.* Many herps cannot tolerate the toxins that get into the water and land, and the chemicals that act like hormones and trick their bodies into not working right.
- *Invasive species.* The animals living in a place adapt to the rest of the species around them. They figure out how to compete with them so they get enough food and shelter, and they develop defenses so predators cannot eat all of them. However, when something new moves into the community all of a sudden, the local herps may not be able to survive. Fire ants, which were accidentally brought into the United States in the 1930s, are one example.
- *Diseases and parasites.* Several diseases are

THE BURMESE PYTHON—A CASE STUDY OF AN INVASIVE SPECIES

South Florida has for many years been a hub of the exotic animal trade in the United States. Its tropical climate is friendly to a variety of reptile species that are popular in the pet trade. With so many exotic reptiles being imported into the Miami area, some escapes (or intentional releases) were inevitable. Each edition of the *Peterson Field Guide to Reptiles and Amphibians of Eastern and Central North America* lists more nonnative species than the previous one, species like the Nile Monitor, Giant Ameiva, Spectacled Caiman, and Burmese Python. This python species is easy to keep in captivity and generally easygoing, and the babies are cute. This made it a popular pet, and many people bought them even though they grow quickly and can reach lengths of at least fifteen feet (and the record length, in captivity, is twenty-seven feet, according to the Peterson guide). As a result, not so many people keep them after they reach adult size, and at least some were released into the wetlands of South Florida by owners who got tired of them or were not prepared to care for a very large snake. Then, in 1992, Hurricane Andrew came ashore south of Miami and destroyed many structures, including those of a wildlife dealer, resulting in the release of many of these pythons. By the year 2000, it was clear that a breeding population of this giant snake was established around the Everglades.

It is often hard to know exactly how much harm an invasive species like this does, but some do a great deal of damage—think of the harm done by the Red Imported Fire Ant, a native of South America accidentally introduced in the United States around 1940. It is thought that the Burmese Python has decimated populations of small mammals such as the opossum, bobcat, and raccoon in South Florida. A 2012 study described how the numbers of these mammals had declined during surveys taken on night drives through back roads. Compared to years prior to the python being established there, sightings declined by anywhere from 88% to 99% in areas where pythons were found. Outside the areas where the snakes were breeding, the counts of such mammals were much higher. The story of the Burmese Python shows how important it is that we never release animals outside of where they are naturally found.

A seventeen-foot Burmese Python removed from South Florida (photo courtesy of National Park Service)

important threats to herps, and three important examples are caused by fungi. One of them has caused significant declines in frogs,[3] and another is affecting salamanders in Europe (and could spread to the United States).[4] A third affects the skin of snakes.[5] These fungi have probably been around for a while, so why are they a problem now? Perhaps they have been spread to new places, or maybe changes in climate or habitat have made herps more vulnerable to them.

- *Unsustainable human use.* People have always used reptiles and amphibians in folk medicine, as food, and as pets. With increasing numbers of people and modern ways of harvesting herps and shipping them across the world, we sometimes take so many that their populations are harmed.

- *Climate change.* Changing patterns of temperature and rainfall affect herps in several ways. For many turtles, the sex of offspring depends on the temperature at which the eggs incubate. As the climate gets warmer, many turtle nests may produce nearly all females and too few males. Additionally, reptiles that are adapted to hunt during the day, such as some lizards, might not be able to survive hotter midday temperatures. If they can hunt only in the morning and evening, they might not find enough food.[6] Examples like this show how climate change can harm herps.

Each of these threats to herps (and to many other kinds of plants and animals) has some connection to human activity. We have some degree of control over each one. If enough of us wanted to, we could make changes in our own behavior that would reduce the threats to wildlife.

Years ago, a TV show (and then a movie) called *Mission:*

Impossible started each episode with a recorded message to a team of secret agents, telling them of some very bad and dangerous situation they could solve, if they chose to accept the mission. Of course they accepted each mission, and because of their skills, training, bravery, and teamwork, they managed to succeed. We look around and see herps disappearing along with the streams, woods, marshes, prairies, and other places they live. The message for us is this: "Your mission, if you choose to accept it, is to speak up for the turtles, snakes, frogs, and other animals." That might mean sharing what we know about the value and beauty of a mountainside forest and the salamanders that live in the streams there. We can introduce people to the complex life of a wetland and change the mental picture of a nasty, useless "swamp" that many people see when they look at wetlands. We can make choices in our own lives that don't add as much to pollution and habitat loss. We can pay attention to the decisions that societies, businesses, and governments make, and speak up to let them know what we think about those choices.

I'm not trying to convince you to be any particular kind of concerned citizen. You don't have to stand on a street corner with a sign, though that can be a powerful way of speaking up. Together we can do a lot just in the way we talk with friends about the things we like and value. For example, you are speaking up for nature when you tell someone about how much you liked a visit to a preserve, or an encounter with an animal. You are speaking up when you attend a presentation about herps or join others for a guided walk at a nature center, even if you hardly say a word. You are making a difference just by being a visible example of someone who values such things.

You can also speak up by supporting organizations that help conserve wildlife and natural places. One such organization is the Orianne Society,[7] which has done much work with the Eastern Indigo Snake and also does habitat restoration in longleaf pine habitats in southeastern states. Their work also includes the Appalachian region and the forests of the northeastern United States, where they focus on species like the Timber Rattlesnake and the Wood Turtle. Another organization you might be interested in is the Turtle Survival Alliance,[8] which operates all over the world with the goal of zero turtle extinctions in the twenty-first century. Another well-known organization that is not as focused on herps is the Nature Conservancy,[9] which protects habitats either by owning them or by working closely with governments, corporations, and landowners to help them protect natural features of their properties. Protecting habitat is probably the single most important way to conserve herps (and the other animals and plants whose lives are all woven together in a place).

You can write to government representatives to let them know how important it is to you that wildlife and wild places be protected, along with clean air and water. If you are not yet old enough to vote, that's OK; you're a citizen of this country and your voice counts. Don't think that your letter has to be perfectly worded or that you must go into lots of scientific detail. Just

The Nature Conservancy's Love Creek Preserve (photo by Rich Kostecke)

know enough about your topic so that what you say is supported by facts. After that, just say what you have to say and send it off to your representative. That's how it is supposed to work, right? Elected officials should want to know what you think, and if enough people agree with you, it could affect the decisions officials make about public lands, wildlife, and the environment.

So that is the mission I am suggesting to you, to be a voice for the wild places in this country and the plants and animals that live in them. Like the characters in *Mission: Impossible*, you have the skills, and you are getting the training. And along with that, I believe you have the bravery and ability to work with others so that you can succeed in this mission. Neither you nor I can save every species or protect every beautiful place. I think that the way to succeed is to move things in the right direction, to spread the word so that more people know of the importance of the natural world. We succeed when another place is protected, when pollution does not get dumped into a waterway, and when a population of reptiles or amphibians still has a place to live this year and the next.

Glossary

Antivenom—(also called "antivenin") A medication used to neutralize snake venom (or that of another venomous animal). It works by attaching itself to venom proteins so that those proteins do not harm the body. Antivenom is given intravenously under close medical supervision.

Carapace—The upper shell of a turtle.

Cloaca—In reptiles, amphibians, and some other animals, the opening at the end of the body where wastes are expelled, eggs are laid (or babies born), and mating takes place.

Constriction—A method of killing prey used by certain snake species, in which several coils of the snake's body are wrapped around the prey animal, and muscle contractions squeeze the animal, preventing blood circulation and breathing.

Dorsolateral ridge—In certain frogs, a ridge of skin on each side of the frog's back running from behind the head to just before the point where the back legs join the body. That ridge contains many glands that secrete mild toxins.

Dry bite—A bite from a venomous snake in which no venom is injected. These snakes (even babies) can control how much venom to inject in a bite and occasionally do not inject venom at all.

Ectothermic—Getting heat from outside the body (as opposed to generating heat within the body).

Genus—A group of living things that are related; a genus may contain a number of species. The gartersnakes and ribbonsnakes are all grouped in one genus.

Hemipenes—Paired copulatory organs (one on each side) ordinarily kept inside the base of the tail of a male snake or lizard. Either one of them would be called a hemipenis.

Hemotoxic—A description of certain snake venoms that act

primarily to break down blood cells, blood vessels, muscle, and other tissue.

Herpetology—The study of reptiles and amphibians, using scientific methods and principles.

Home range—The area within which an individual animal generally stays, mking use of the food, water, and shelter found there. Many herps will, if moved, attempt to return to that location by using cues such as the position of the sun or the earth's geomagnetic field.

Hypothesis—A proposed explanation for something, based on the information we already have (like an educated guess about why something happens).

Larva—(plural: larvae) An immature form of an animal that will later transform into a different form; for example, tadpoles are larvae of frogs.

Metamorphosis—A transformation from one form to another, such as the change from an aquatic larval form of an amphibian to an air-breathing adult form.

Neurotoxic—A description of certain snake venoms that primarily interfere with nerve transmission, resulting in symptoms such as respiratory arrest or paralysis.

Nictitating membrane—A clear (or nearly clear) membrane under an animal's external eyelid that can close across the eye to protect or moisturize the eye while still allowing the animal to see.

Osteoderm—Bony material within a scale, such as are found on the American Alligator or Gila Monster. Osteoderms strengthen the scales like a suit of armor.

Parotoid Gland—An external skin gland on a toad, frog, or salamander that secretes toxic substances that discourage predators. These glands are particularly obvious on toads, as raised lumps on the skin on the back of the toad's head.

Plastron—The lower shell of a turtle.

Quadrate—A bone at the back of the skull of birds or reptiles, to which the lower jaw is attached. In snakes, the quadrate is movable where it attaches to the skull, as well as where it attaches to the jaw. That allows the mouth to have a larger gape when the snake eats large prey animals.

Snake hook—A piece of equipment for maneuvering snakes and for lifting objects without putting your fingers under the object. It has a handle about the length of a golf club, with a hook at the end shaped like an L to slide under and lift a snake or a rock, log, or piece of tin. Some people make their own snake hooks, but strong and lightweight hooks are available commercially.

Species—Organisms that share common characteristics and can typically breed with each other and produce fertile offspring. The Plains Gartersnake is a different species than the Wandering Gartersnake.

Spermatophore—A small packet containing sperm, deposited by some male salamanders so the female can pick it up into her cloaca to fertilize eggs.

Subspecies—If a population of a particular species in one location is significantly different from a population of that species somewhere else (but they are all the same species), they may be classified as different subspecies. The Terrestrial Gartersnakes found from New Mexico to Montana and Idaho are a subspecies called the Wandering Gartersnake, but one of the populations in California and Oregon is called the Mountain Gartersnake.

Tadpole—The larval form of a frog; an aquatic stage of the frog's life between hatching from an egg and developing into a mature frog.

Thermoregulation—The process of regulating temperature within an acceptable range, such as by moving into sunlight to warm up or into shade to cool off.

Vomeronasal organ (Jacobson's organ)—A sense organ in the roof of the mouth of some animals that detects chemical signals similar to odors. This organ is particularly well developed in snakes and some lizards.

Notes

Chapter 1

1. M. A. Smith and C. R. King, *Herping Texas: The Quest for Reptiles and Amphibians* (College Station: Texas A&M University Press, 2018).

2. G. M. Burghardt, "Chemical Preference Studies on Newborn Snakes of Three Sympatric Species of *Natrix*," *Copeia* (1968): 732–37.

3. "All about Herps!," Society for the Study of Amphibians and Reptiles, accessed July 8, 2018, https://ssarherps.org/all-about-herps/.

4. Center for North American Herpetology, accessed July 8, 2018, http://www.cnah.org.

5. iNaturalist, accessed January 13, 2019, https://www.inaturalist.org.

Chapter 2

1. P. Young, *Tortoise* (London: Reaktion Books, 2003), 42–45.

2. "Wikipedia: Rod of Asclepius," Wikimedia Foundation, accessed July 21, 2018, https://en.wikipedia.org/wiki/Rod_of_Asclepius.

3. L. M. Klauber, *Rattlesnakes: Their Habits, Life Histories, and Influence on Mankind*, abridged (Berkeley: University of California Press, 1982), 279–82.

4. R. M. DeGraaff, *The Book of the Toad* (Rochester, VT: Park Street Press, 1991), 141–43.

5. "What Does It Mean to Be Human?," Smithsonian National Museum of Natural History, accessed July 14, 2018, http://humanorigins.si.edu/evidence/human-fossils/species/homo-sapiens.

6. "Dinosaurs Were Discovered by British Scientists," BBC Earth, accessed July 14, 2018, http://www.bbc.com/earth/story/20150603-the-land-that-gave-us-dinosaurs.

7. "Seymouria," *Encyclopaedia Brittanica*, accessed July 20, 2019, https://www.britannica.com/animal/Seymouria.

8. "Wikipedia: *Dimetrodon*," Wikimedia Foundation, accessed July 14, 2018, https://en.wikipedia.org/wiki/Dimetrodon.

9. A. Bellairs, *The Life of Reptiles* (New York: Universe Books, 1970), 1:22.

Chapter 3

1. F. H. Pough, R. M. Andrews, J. E. Cadle, M. L. Crump, A. H. Savitzky, and K. D. Wells, *Herpetology* (Upper Saddle River, NJ: Prentice-Hall, 1998), 210, 365–66.

2. J. W. Gibbons and M. E. Dorcas, *North American Watersnakes: A Natural History* (Norman: University of Oklahoma Press, 2004), 96.

3. C. H. Ernst and J. E. Lovich, *Turtles of the United States and Canada*, 2nd ed. (Baltimore: Johns Hopkins University Press, 2009), 132–33.

4. Carl Franklin, personal communication.

5. T. D. Hibbitts and T. L. Hibbitts, *Texas Turtles and Crocodilians: A Field Guide* (Austin: University of Texas Press, 2016), 107.

Chapter 4

1. C. H. Ernst and G. R. Zug, *Snakes in Question* (Washington, DC: Smithsonian Institution Press, 1996), 17.

2. Bellairs, *Life of Reptiles*, 2:382–84.

3. J. E. Werler and J. R. Dixon, *Texas Snakes: Identification, Distribution, and Natural History* (Austin: University of Texas Press, 2000), 119–20.

4. R. C. Stebbins and N. W. Cohen, *A Natural History of Amphibians* (Princeton, NJ: Princeton University Press, 1995), 98.

5. Stebbins and Cohen, 78–79.

6. L. Elliott, C. Gerhardt, and C. Davidson, 2009. *The Frogs and Toads of North America: A Comprehensive Guide to Their Identification, Behavior, and Calls* (Boston: Houghton Mifflin Harcourt, 2009).

Chapter 5

1. Werler and Dixon, *Texas Snakes*, 362.

2. Werler and Dixon, 363.

3. Adam Britton, "Integumentary Sense Organs," Crocodilian Biology Database, accessed May 25, 2019, http://crocodilian.com/cnhc/cbd-gb1.htm.

4. Ernst and Lovich, *Turtles of the United States and Canada*, 446.

5. M. J. Acierno, M. A. Mitchell, M. K. Roundtree, and T. T. Zachariah, "Effects of Ultraviolet Radiation on 25-Hydroxyvitamin D_3 Synthesis in Red-eared Slider Turtles (*Trachemys scripta elegans*)." *American Journal of Veterinary Research* 67, no. 12 (2006): 2046–49.

6. R. Orenstein, *Turtles, Tortoises, and Terrapins: Survivors in Armor* (Buffalo, NY: Firefly Books, 2001), 131.

7. L. J. Vitt and J. P. Caldwell, *Herpetology: An Introductory Biology of Amphibians and Reptiles*, 4th ed. (Amsterdam: Elsevier, 2014), 212.

8. J. W. Petranka, *Salamanders of the United States and Canada* (Washington, DC: Smithsonian Books, 1998), 89.

Chapter 6

1. D. E. Brown and N. B. Carmony, *Gila Monster: Facts and Folklore of America's Aztec Lizard* (Salt Lake City: University of Utah Press, 1999), 40–41.

2. Brown and Carmony, 39.

3. Stebbins and Cohen, *Natural History of Amphibians*, 105–6.

4. B. L. Tipton, T. L. Hibbitts, T. D. Hibbitts, T. J. Hibbitts, and T. J. LaDuc, *Texas Amphibians: A Field Guide* (Austin: University of Texas Press, 2012), 245.

5. M. A. Dimmitt and R. Ruibal, "Environmental Correlates of Emergence in Spadefoot Toads (*Scaphiopus*)," *Journal of Herpetology* 14, no. 1 (1980): 21–29.

6. "*Scaphiopus couchii*," AmphibiaWeb, accessed December 18, 2018, https://amphibiaweb.org/cgi/amphib_query?where-genus=Scaphiopus&where-species=couchii&account=lannoo.

Chapter 7

1. C. H. Ernst, *Venomous Reptiles of North America* (Washington, DC: Smithsonian Institution Press, 1992), 50–51.

2. M. Rubio, *Rattlesnake: Portrait of a Predator* (Washington, DC: Smithsonian Institution Press, 1998), 52–56.

3. R. Powell, R. Conant, and J. T. Collins. 2016. *Peterson Field Guide to Reptiles and Amphibians of Eastern and Central North America*, 4th ed. (New York: Houghton Mifflin Harcourt, 2016), 439.

4. W. L. Hodges, "Texas Horned Lizard," in *Lizards of the American Southwest: A Photographic Field Guide*, ed. L. L. C. Jones and R. E. Lovich (Tucson, AZ: Rio Nuevo, 2009), 168.

5. B. Smith, "How the Texas Horned Lizard Harvests Water on Its Skin." *Cosmos*, accessed January 12, 2019, https://cosmosmagazine.com/biology/how-texas-horned-lizard-harvests-water-its-skin.

6. Hodges, "Texas Horned Lizard."

7. J. Manaster, *Horned Lizards* (Austin: University of Texas Press, 1997), 27.

8. W. C. Sherbrooke, *Introduction to Horned Lizards of North America* (Berkeley: University of California Press, 2003), 127–28.

9. S. Leland, *Where Did the Horny Toad Go?*, Jar of Grasshoppers Productions (2012), accessed July 20, 2019, https://vimeo.com/jarofgrasshopper.

10. C. K. Dodd, *North American Box Turtles: A Natural History* (Norman: University of Oklahoma Press, 2001), 192.

Chapter 8

1. J. R. Dixon, *Amphibians and Reptiles of Texas*, 3rd ed. (College Station: Texas A&M University Press, 2013).

2. R. C. Stebbins and S. M. McGinnis, *Peterson Field Guide to Western Reptiles and Amphibians*, 4th ed. (New York: Houghton Mifflin, 2018).

3. Powell, Conant, and Collins, *Peterson Field Guide*.

4. D. A. Pike, B. M. Croak, J. K. Webb, and R. Shine, "Subtle— but Easily Reversible—Anthropogenic Disturbance Seriously

Degrades Habitat Quality for Rock-Dwelling Reptiles," *Animal Conservation* 13 (2010): 411–18.

5. "Endangered Species," US Fish and Wildlife Service, accessed August 16, 2018, https://www.fws.gov/endangered/species/us-species.html.

6. E. R. Jacobson, "Implications of Infectious Diseases for Captive Propagation and Introduction Programs of Threatened/Endangered Reptiles," *Journal of Zoo and Wildlife Medicine* 24, no. 3 (1993): 245–55.

Chapter 9

1. "Getting Started," iNaturalist, accessed January 25, 2019, https://www.inaturalist.org/pages/getting+started.

2. D. E. Keyler, "Envenomation and First Aid," in *Venomous Snakebite in the Western United States*, ed. M. Rubio and D. E. Keyler (Rodeo, NM: ECO Herpetological Publishing, 2013), 8.

3. E. J. Lavonas, A. Ruha, W. Banner, V. Bebarta, J. N. Bernstein, S. P. Bush, W. P. Kerns, et al., "Unified Treatment Algorithm for the Management of Crotaline Snakebite in the United States: Results of an Evidence-Informed Consensus Workshop," *BMC Emergency Medicine* 11, no. 2 (2011), accessed July 19, 2019, https://bmcemergmed.biomedcentral.com/articles/10.1186/1471-227X-11-2.

4. D. A. Tanen, A. Ruha, K. A. Graeme, and S. C. Curry, "Epidemiology and Hospital Course of Rattlesnake Envenomations Cared for at a Tertiary Referral Center in Central Arizona," *Academic Emergency Medicine* 8, no. 2 (2001): 177–82.

5. M. McMillen, "How to Survive Snake Season, Even If You Get Bitten," WebMD, accessed January 25, 2019, https://www.webmd.com/first-aid/news/20180525/how-to-survive-snake-season-even-if-you-get-bitten.

6. N. C. Kanaan, J. Ray, M. Stewart, K. W. Russell, M. Fuller, S. P. Bush, E. M. Caravati, et al., "Wilderness Medical Society Practice Guidelines for the Treatment of Pitviper Envenomations in the United States and Canada," *Wilderness and Environmental Medicine* 26 (2015): 472–87.

7. S. P. Bush, "Snakebite Suction Devices Don't Remove Venom: They Just Suck," *Annals of Emergency Medicine* 43, no. 2 (2004): 187–88.

8. Lavonas et al., "Unified Treatment Algorithm."

9. "SnakeBite911 Apps," BTG International, accessed January 25, 2019, https://www.crofab.com/SnakeBite911/SnakeBite911.

Chapter 10

1. J. E. Lovich, J. R. Ennen, M. Agha, and J. W. Gibbons, "Where Have All the Turtles Gone, and Why Does It Matter?," *BioScience* 68, no. 10 (2018): 771–81.

2. J. W. Gibbons, D. E. Scott, T. J. Ryan, K. A. Buhlmann, T. D. Tuberville, B. S. Metts, J. L. Greene, et al., "The Global Decline of Reptiles, Déjà Vu Amphibians," *BioScience* 50, no. 8 (2000): 653–66.

3. "Chytrid Fungus," Amphibian Ark, accessed December 22, 2018, http://www.amphibianark.org/the-crisis/chytrid-fungus/.

4. "*Batrachochytrium salamandrivorans*: Deadly Fungal Threat to Salamanders," AmphibiaWeb, accessed December 22, 2018, https://amphibiaweb.org/chytrid/Bsal.html.

5. J. M. Lorch, S. Knowles, J. S. Lankton, K. Michell, J. L. Edwards, J. M. Kapfer, R. A. Staffen, et al., "Snake Fungal Disease: An Emerging Threat to Wild Snakes," *Philosophical Transactions of the Royal Society of London, Series B, Biological Sciences* 371, no. 1709 (2016): 20150457.

6. B. Sinervo, F. Méndez-de-la-Cruz, D. B. Miles, B. Heulin, E. Bastiaans, M. Villagrán-Santa Cruz, R. Lara-Resendiz, et al., "Erosion of Lizard Diversity by Climate Change and Altered Thermal Niches," *Science* 328 (2010): 894–99.

7. Orianne Society, accessed December 25, 2018, https://www.oriannesociety.org.

8. Turtle Survival Alliance, accessed December 26, 2018, https://turtlesurvival.org.

9. The Nature Conservancy, accessed December 25, 2018, https://www.nature.org/en-us/.

Bibliography

Bellairs, A. 1970. *The Life of Reptiles*. Vols. 1 and 2. New York: Universe Books.

Brown, D. E., and N. B. Carmony. 1999. *Gila Monster: Facts and Folklore of America's Aztec Lizard*. Salt Lake City: University of Utah Press.

Carroll, D. M. 1991. *The Year of the Turtle*. New York: St. Martin's Griffin.

DeGraaff, R. M. 1991. *The Book of the Toad*. Rochester, VT: Park Street Press.

Dixon, J. R. 2013. *Amphibians and Reptiles of Texas*. 3rd ed. College Station: Texas A&M University Press.

Dodd, C. K. 2001. *North American Box Turtles: A Natural History*. Norman: University of Oklahoma Press.

Elliott, L., C. Gerhardt, and C. Davidson. 2009. *The Frogs and Toads of North America: A Comprehensive Guide to Their Identification, Behavior, and Calls*. Boston: Houghton Mifflin Harcourt.

Ernst, C. H. 1992. *Venomous Reptiles of North America*. Washington, DC: Smithsonian Institution Press.

Ernst, C. H., and J. E. Lovich. 2009. *Turtles of the United States and Canada*. 2nd ed. Baltimore: Johns Hopkins University Press.

Ernst, C. H., and G. R. Zug. 1996. *Snakes in Question*. Washington, DC: Smithsonian Institution Press.

Gibbons, J. W., and M. E. Dorcas. 2004. *North American Watersnakes: A Natural History*. Norman: University of Oklahoma Press.

Greene, H. W. 1997. *Snakes: The Evolution of Mystery in Nature*. Berkeley: University of California Press.

Hibbitts, T. D., and T. L. Hibbitts. 2015. *Texas Lizards: A Field Guide*. Austin: University of Texas Press.

———. 2016. *Texas Turtles and Crocodilians: A Field Guide*. Austin: University of Texas Press.

Hodges, W. L. 2009. "Texas Horned Lizard." In *Lizards of the American Southwest: A Photographic Field Guide*, edited by L. L. C. Jones and R. E. Lovich. Tucson, AZ: Rio Nuevo.

Jones, L. L. C., and R. E. Lovich, eds. 2009. *Lizards of the American Southwest: A Photographic Field Guide*. Tucson, AZ: Rio Nuevo.

Keyler, D. E. 2013. "Envenomation and First Aid." In *Venomous Snakebite in the Western United States*, edited by M. Rubio and D. E. Keyler. Rodeo, NM: ECO Herpetological Publishing.

Klauber, L. M. 1982. *Rattlesnakes: Their Habits, Life Histories, and Influence on Mankind*. Abridged. Berkeley: University of California Press.

Maginnis, T. L. 2006. "The Costs of Autotomy and Regeneration in Animals: A Review and Framework for Future Research," *Behavioral Ecology* 17 (5): 857–72.

Manaster, J. 1997. *Horned Lizards*. Austin: University of Texas Press.

Orenstein, R. 2001. *Turtles, Tortoises, and Terrapins: Survivors in Armor*. Buffalo, NY: Firefly Books.

Petranka, J. W. 1998. *Salamanders of the United States and Canada*. Washington, DC: Smithsonian Books.

Pianka, E. R., and L. J. Vitt. 2003. *Lizards: Windows to the Evolution of Diversity*. Berkeley: University of California Press.

Pough, F. H., R. M. Andrews, J. E. Cadle, M. L. Crump, A. H. Savitzky, and K. D. Wells. 1998. *Herpetology*. Upper Saddle River, NJ: Prentice-Hall.

Powell, R., R. Conant, and J. T. Collins. 2016. *Peterson Field Guide to Reptiles and Amphibians of Eastern and Central North America*. 4th ed. New York: Houghton Mifflin Harcourt.

Price, A. H. 2009. *Venomous Snakes of Texas: A Field Guide*. Austin: University of Texas Press.

Rubio, M. 1998. *Rattlesnake: Portrait of a Predator*. Washington, DC: Smithsonian Institution Press.

Sherbrooke, W. C. 2003. *Introduction to Horned Lizards of North America*. Berkeley: University of California Press.

Smith, M. A., and C. R. King. 2018. *Herping Texas: The Quest for Reptiles and Amphibians*. College Station: Texas A&M University Press.

Stebbins, R. C., and N. W. Cohen. 1995. *A Natural History of Amphibians*. Princeton, NJ: Princeton University Press.

Stebbins, R. C., and S. M. McGinnis. 2018. *Peterson Field Guide to Western Reptiles and Amphibians*. 4th ed. New York: Houghton Mifflin.

Tipton, B. L., T. L. Hibbitts, T. D. Hibbitts, T. J. Hibbitts, and T. J. LaDuc. 2012. *Texas Amphibians: A Field Guide*. Austin: University of Texas Press.

Vitt, L. J., and J. P. Caldwell. 2014. *Herpetology: An Introductory Biology of Amphibians and Reptiles*. 4th ed. London: Academic Press.

Werler, J. E., and J. R. Dixon. 2000. *Texas Snakes: Identification, Distribution, and Natural History*. Austin: University of Texas Press.

Young, P. 2003. *Tortoise*. London: Reaktion Books.

Index

DeGraaff, Robert, 14–15
Dekay's Brownsnake, 89
Denver Museum of Nature & Science, 18
desert habitat, 63–73
diamond-backed rattlesnakes, 1, 2, 74–77, 80–82
Dimetrodon, 16
Dimmitt, Mark, 72
dinosaurs, reptiles' relationship to, 11, 16–19
diseases and parasites that affect herps, 117, 120
dorsolateral ridge, frog, 23, 125
Doyle, Arthur Conan, 15
dragons, 17
drinking, frog-style, 71
"dry bite" from venomous snake, 113, 125

Eastern Coachwhip, 70
Eastern Diamond-backed Rattlesnake, 82
Eastern Ratsnake, 39
eating, snake method, 39, 78–80
ectothermic property of herps, 4–5, 40–41, 125
Elliott, Lang, 43
eyes, snakes', 35, 77

fangs, 50–51
fence lizards, 89
field herpetology
  benefits of, 116
  catching and collecting considerations, 95–100
  conservation ethic, 116–23
  dangers of returning collected animals to the wild, 101–2
  flipping herp cover (rock, tin, wood), 93–94
  getting started in, 8–10, 89–102
  how-to advice, 92–95

planning your trip, 103–6, 110–12
purpose and love for, 116–23
recording and sharing observations, 106–10
safety tips, 94, 110–15
searching techniques, 92–95
species and habitat knowledge, 90–91
time in the field, 90
venomous snakebite guidance, 112–15
field notes, keeping, 106–9
fire ants, 85
Five-Lined Skink, 100
flipping objects to find herps, 93–94
folk tales and myths about reptiles and amphibians, 11–17
freezing temperatures, frogs that survive, 41–42
frogs and toads
as amphibians, 4–5
  bullfrogs, 27, *106*
  calling by, 42–43
  chorus frogs, 8, 42
  Cricket Frogs, 28, 43
  Green Frog, 43
  Leopard Frog, 21–24
  in mythology, 14–15
  spadefoot toads, 70–73
  tadpole-to-frog process, 20–24
  treefrogs, 40–43
The Frogs and Toads of North America (Elliott), 43

gartersnakes, 3, 74, 96
genus, 6, 7, 125
Gila Monster, 63–66
Graham's Crawfish Snake, 6
grasslands (Great Plains), 74–88
Gray Fox, 84–85
Gray Ratsnake, 39
Gray Treefrog, 40–43
Greater Short-horned Lizard, 85
Great Plains habitat, 74–88